MAKE TH
MONEY COUNT

Darren Laverty

WRITE BUSINESS RESULTS

This book was produced in collaboration with Write Business Results Ltd. www.writebusinessresults.com info@writebusinessresults.com

"For any employer who truly wants to make a positive difference and improve the financial literacy of their employees, this book is a must read. Well done Darren for sharing your colourful insights to brighten up a grey financial world!"

John Hoffmire - Director Impact Bond Fund – University of Oxford

"This book is all very logical and easy to understand – a robust starting point for any company who hasn't yet set off on a path of financial wellbeing for their employees.

Gemma Isaac - Vice President People & Organisation, EMEA – Sony Pictures

"There's a lot of coverage both about what employee financial well-being is (or isn't) and why it's important for workers, employers, society and government. However, there's not been as much attention given to how it can be delivered. Based on a wealth of personal experience and the latest insights from behavioural science, this book helps fills the gap giving practical guidance to those wanting to implement an effective workplace financial well-being strategy."

Charles Cotton - Performance and Reward Adviser to the The Chartered Institute of Personnel and Development

This book is dedicated to two schools in Kenya that I fell in love with in 2011, The Amani Junior Academy & the Showers of Blessings Academy. All profits from the sale of this book go to them.

Special thanks to Michelle Bradshaw. It is her vision and pioneering spirit that has enabled the contents of this book to be developed and tested in the real world.

Contents

Introduction

Wellbeing is a word that's used a lot nowadays and covers a multitude of things. There's physical wellbeing, psychological wellbeing and, the one that I believe underpins the other two, financial wellbeing.

The world of financial planning has changed dramatically in the past 30 years. Retirement has become more complex, wage increases have stalled, the cost of living has climbed and savings have been eroded. Family wealth is tied up in property, and young people are entering the workplace with unprecedented levels of debt from education.

Unsecured debt is on the rise again and almost half of employees in large organisations admit to being stressed about money, so it's very clear that many employees do not have that valuable sense of financial wellbeing and would definitely derive benefit from guidance and education on how to make their financial lives and their financial futures feel more safe and secure.

But what exactly is financial wellbeing? It basically comes down to feeling a sense of financial freedom; being in a position where you can make the best choices for your health, lifestyle, and happiness without being held back by financial insecurity and anxiety. Through my work talking to thousands of employees over the last 20+ years, I know that this is the ultimate goal in terms of money. Everybody wants to feel financially free.

Introducing a workplace financial wellbeing strategy is one way to help achieve this sense of financial freedom. Its purpose is to help employees make the right decisions with their money, reduce their debt and ultimately grow their personal wealth. When you have that sense of freedom, instead of worrying about money, you're able to focus your attention on your physical and psychological wellbeing.

The more employees we introduce to workplace financial wellbeing strategies, the more happy, healthy, productive, engaged and innovative they become. Who wouldn't want a workforce that looks like that?

As an employer, keeping everyone happy is a difficult balancing act. You're juggling many balls and your employees' wellbeing is just one of them. But have you considered that by focusing on employee wellbeing, and particularly their financial freedom, that it could become a little easier to juggle those remaining balls of company performance and profitability?

I've experienced the power of a financial wellbeing strategy first hand, seen the power it has to improve people's lives through my work and want more people at every stage of their careers to tap into this tool to improve every aspect of their lives and make them happier.

This book will help you understand the importance of financial wellbeing strategies on an organisational level, and look at why they have a positive impact on people's lives away from their finances.

I'm also going to explain the four stages of a successful financial wellbeing strategy that we have found to work most effectively through our decades of experience and knowledge. I'll be delving into why each stage is beneficial from a personal perspective and how that translates into your organisation.

The focus of this book is on improving the how and less about the what and the why. The 'what' employees need educating on is fairly easy to work out, getting them to learn and take action is the challenging bit. I'm going to expose you to the most overlooked but important aspects of a financial education strategy - the parts most people don't even know exist.

1 A Fresh Perspective On Workplace Wellbeing

Workplace wellbeing is not a new concept

In the late 1900s the Cadbury family moved their chocolate production factory to a rural area called Bournebrook Hall, six miles south of Birmingham. The family were very concerned about the wellbeing of their employees so they set about building a community and a lifestyle for them. They treated their workers very respectfully, paying high wages and building 313 houses. They called the area Bourneville Village.

They were given good conditions to work in, with pension schemes, works committees and a full medical service provided. They were concerned about their employees' health and fitness so they created parks and recreational areas and actively encouraged swimming, walking and outdoor sports. They built a football pitch, hockey pitch, several bowling greens, a fishing lake and a swimming lido. All these facilities were available to the workers and their families free of charge.

It appears that we can learn a lot from the past. Most employers today are simply unable to provide anywhere near the same sort of workplace environment for their employees. Although, if money was no object I believe most HR people would love to provide these sorts of facilities.

Today we are seeing a trend towards this type of employee wellbeing experience where it is possible. The focus on introducing physical wellbeing strategies seems to have run its course and attention has shifted to psychological and financial wellbeing. By addressing financial wellbeing, there is obviously a positive impact on the psychological side too because it can help reduce financial worries and stress.

In addition, government recognition of the importance of financial wellbeing has now developed into policy by safeguarding wages through George Osborne's 'National Living Wage' initiative which saw the minimum wage increase to £7.20 per hour for over 25 year olds. As well as the government minimum wage increasing further in 2017, a whole host of businesses have joined forces with the 'Living Wage Foundation' to ensure a 'real' living wage that promotes employee financial wellbeing, which is £8.45 per hour outside of London and £9.75 within it. This is acknowledgement at the highest level of the importance of wages in creating and maintaining a content workforce.

The responsibility of financial wellbeing, especially when it comes to employees' retirement, was originally taken care of by employers and the government. Due to economic factors over the last decade plus a whole host of legislative changes to do with pension schemes, the responsibility has transferred to individual employees. The main problem with this is that the vast majority do not have the knowledge, confidence or tools to deal with the complexity of their finances.

The first issue to be addressed, therefore, is employees' understanding of all things financial. This transfer of responsibility at a time of unprecedented complexity, coupled with the lack of financial education resources, is a big driver of a workplace financial education strategy.

Where have the all the financial educators gone?

If we look back 25 or 30 years there was a much stronger culture of saving. I remember in the 70s, the Trustee Savings Bank would visit our school every Friday and us pupils would line up and deposit our weekly two bob into our savings account. We would compete with each other at age six or seven as to who had saved the most. I remember after a whole school year reaching the milestone of £3.

Also, at that time there were many people in financial services, albeit with a very basic level of expertise, known as life insurance agents or 'the man from the Pru' types. They basically persuaded people to buy life insurance for their families and to start monthly payment medium-term saving plans to provide a buffer in the future when they may have a slightly more complex and expensive lifestyle, often to smooth out the reduction in income when a parent ceased working due to having children. As a concept this was a group of people providing a community service. Where is the harm in saving money and insuring yourself?

At the peak, there were in excess of 300,000 of these individuals going out, meeting ordinary people and 'educating' them of the importance of saving and insuring. These individuals slowly disappeared through changes to the industry. Much of this change was driven by the low quality of the products, which were often not good value, and the qualifications of the agents (later to become financial advisers). However, what our country had was 300,000 financial 'educators' helping millions of people save for the future and creating good habits that would serve them for their whole lives. Overall, I believe the good outweighed the bad. Why do I say that? It's based on an experience I had in 1998.

I started in the industry as a 'life insurance agent' in the 80s, and it was at this time that I met Stuart. In 1988, at the age of 19, he started a savings plan with me. He did it because I had educated him about the importance of saving. 10 years later, that savings plan matured and I arranged to meet him to present him with his payout cheque. What we both realised very quickly was that the amount of the cheque was less than the total amount of money invested. You can imagine my embarrassment!

I apologised and immediately tried to think of ways to compensate him. He then amazed me by saying that this was money that he would never have had if it wasn't for me educating him 10 years earlier and getting him into his savings habit. In fact, he pointed out that he had accumulated other savings and also bought two properties during that period. He put it down to me catching him early and creating this good habit of saving that he would never stop.

Stuart is now 47 and has retired due to his lifetime habit of saving. I bet there are countless great stories out there like this, but unfortunately we only get to hear about the bad ones.

The number of 'educators' in society has now dwindled to a fraction of the heady days of the 80s. There are around 23,000 financial advisers in the UK, only about half of which are authorised to arrange investment products[1]. That's about one investment adviser for approx. every 6,000 people. In the 80s it was about one for every 200 people. Advisers are now all professionally qualified and highly regulated, and as a result they are out of reach for most people.

The industry switched its focus away from savings products and followed the profit which is now in credit. The 'flexible friend' was introduced to the UK in the 70s and we are now in a crazy situation where it is easier for somebody to get a credit card than it is for them to take out a savings plan, a recipe for disaster, as we have seen over the last decade. The 'educators' have gone up market, only really supporting people who already have a lot of money and require help organising it, making it grow and last.

[1] Figure extracted from FCA register, Feb 2017

In terms of education for people who do not possess lots of money yet or those who need education to help them to make good decisions such as saving or clearing debt, the responsibility has shifted to employers. Whilst many have been a little slow on the uptake because it has historically been seen as a 'nice to have' rather than a 'must', we are now experiencing the impact the lack of education in recent years has had on employee wellbeing and ultimately productivity and profitability.

It is not a legal requirement, however, many employers are seeing workplace financial education increasingly as a business imperative and an integral part of a wider employee wellbeing strategy. The role of financial educator that was once provided by the 'life insurance agents', has transitioned slowly over to employers and there is now a good business case to justify it.

What is financial freedom?

Well, the obvious answer is that you have enough cash and assets generating sufficient income to support the lifestyle you desire. But what about the vast majority of us who are not that fortunate? Could we create at least a sense of financial freedom before it actually becomes a reality?

I believe the answer is yes. Even wealthy people are not totally worry free, they worry about losing their money, rather than not having it in the first place. However, they do generally feel a strong sense of financial freedom because they feel in control of most things financial in their lives. This means they are better placed to deal with the things life throws at them, especially financial shocks.

Imagine how well your business would perform if the majority of your workforce, irrespective of their financial situation, had a strong sense of personal financial freedom. Imagine that they awaken each day and do not immediately think about money. Money is a strong draw and can steal the attention of employees from the other areas of their lives. Free from this worry, they can focus their attention and energy towards doing the best job they possibly can at work, towards their own personal development inside and out of work. Imagine how creative and innovative they could be if they had this sense of personal financial freedom. They could have more brain space to engage at a deeper level with their employer, their role and their responsibilities.

Is this possible even if they do not possess the wealth? I believe it is. If we can put employees in control of the majority of their finances and provide them with a life plan to focus on, they can feel a sense of financial freedom now and along their journey, rather than always feeling anxiety until they eventually achieve it in reality.

Stress comes from the fear of feeling of out of control. Helping employees take control of their finances will reduce their fears, worries and uncertainties. We then have the foundation to develop a sense of financial freedom which will have a positive impact on all other aspects of their lives.

Employees struggle to keep up with change

We have experienced an unprecedented pace of change in the area of personal finance over the last decade. In the first part of the 2000s we seemed to be flying high, we had seen a long stock market bull run, property had done really well during the same period and people generally felt more secure and certain about their future. Wage inflation outstripped goods and services, which created more disposable income and a stronger feel good factor when compared to today.

Then in 2008, we experienced the financial crisis and everything started to change. Since then, wage rises have been subdued at best and the cost of living has increased, which has put a squeeze on our lifestyles. This situation can impact on employees' wellbeing and state of mind, which isn't good for business.

Interest rates have been at an all time low for many years and this has slowed the growth of cash and helped increase the value of property, leaving families in a situation where it is difficult to access their wealth. For many people these changes in society and our financial lives are being felt very strongly, however, acknowledgment and understanding of what is actually going on is low.

Headcount freezes, along with leavers' roles and responsibilities being absorbed into others has left many employees feeling as though they're working harder than ever before. Not only is this leaving them with less time and energy to focus on their money, we have experienced an inordinate level of change in the world of finance, most of which has gone unnoticed by the majority of people who are unaware of the potential impact of this on their lives.

How can I be so sure? When I present to employees I ask them questions about changes to pensions freedom legislation, interest rates, taxation, savings, etc. The vast majority simply do not know what is going on! Many of them are just running too fast to notice what is happening around them. It certainly feels odd to me that people miss these things, but they are firmly on my radar because it is what I do, I work in the industry. Your employees do not.

In this complicated world with so much more stimulation from technology, social media, work pressures and family stealing our attention, much of the information people require has gone unnoticed, it's under their radar. I believe the role of a good financial education programme is to help employees tune into what is going on. To stop for a moment and become aware of the aspects of finance that are important and relevant to them.

We need to trigger their Reticular Activating System (RAS) so that they notice more, are aware of more and therefore make better decisions. Once stimulated, it can become your employees' personal finance radar.

What is the RAS?

The RAS is part of the brain that filters out the wealth of unnecessary information sent by our five senses. To get by day to day we don't need to be aware of everything all of the time. If we were, our brains would be working overtime and probably fail us. By way of an example, whilst reading this book I bet that you're not aware of the sensation of your clothing touching your skin right at this moment. Well you are now because I have just mentioned it! The RAS in action.

Some people think others are lucky, but I believe that much of this so called luck is actually a result of a more sensitive radar. People who have clearly defined goals sometimes seem lucky in life, but it is their focus on their goals that puts those things that can help them firmly on their radar.

We have learned that a well delivered financial education programme will put financial freedom, financial planning and new found financial information at the forefront of people's minds. Their financial radar is now working and as they go through life they will notice and observe more situations and opportunities that can help them achieve what they want financially opportunities they would probably have missed before. This awareness will help them become more financially savvy and hopefully lead to better decisions in the future.

Being in the financial services industry myself, I always notice financial information on the news and through social media. My radar is highly sensitive in this area and my goal is to 'tune in' my clients' employees to help them and their families enjoy a more prosperous and financially free life.

Transform limiting beliefs

Too many employees have developed a range of limiting beliefs when it comes to financial matters. These manifest themselves in statements such as:

- I don't believe in pensions
- I don't have the time to sort my finances
- I can't afford to save
- I won't be happy until I have a lot of money

- It's not the most important area for me to focus on right now
- Financial education is complicated/boring

However, these statements are rarely the truth. They are most often a story that employees give themselves to protect themselves from something else, usually something they fear. By repeating these stories to themselves, they become a strongly held belief. A good financial education programme has the ability to change these limiting beliefs into empowering beliefs. A half-hearted, poorly delivered financial education programme will simply confirm and reinforce these limiting beliefs.

Imagine your employees went through a financial education programme and transformed their beliefs to the following:

- There is a way out of my financial problems and to feel financially free
- Pensions are the most tax-efficient savings vehicle in the UK
- Pensions are very flexible
- I can easily afford to increase my savings by a few pounds each day
- A stitch in time saves nine when it comes to financial planning
- I can't afford not to save
- If I have a sense of financial freedom I can be happy right now
- Financial education can be fun if it's relevant and delivered well.

To change employees' beliefs we must deliver the content in a way that is more congruent with these empowering beliefs than it is with their limiting beliefs. Basically, the person with more positive conviction – or the most confident and informed communicator - will always influence the person with a lower degree of confidence and a negative conviction. It is a kind of leadership that, directed positively, is exactly what employees require to help them overcome limiting beliefs about money.

FINANCIAL LEADERSHIP

I know this because employees challenge me all the time. There are usually one or two very vocal people who like to publicly challenge a position, but it is very unlikely that they have as much experience as me. I find in almost every reasonable situation, a calm response delivered respectfully wins the day. If what you are saying is not congruent with the way you are saying it, i.e. you lack conviction, people will cling to their limiting beliefs and your apparent lack of belief in what you're saying can make those limiting beliefs stronger.

Focus = feeling

Where focus goes, energy flows. Many education programmes point out problems more than they offer solutions. If we focus employees on the negative and they look at it for long enough they will become unhappy. From a psychological standpoint, staring at problems or visualising an outcome we don't want is a recipe for unhappiness. Sometimes we can't change our situation, but we can change how we feel about it. Everything has more than one perspective and if intelligently used can serve us rather than hinder us.

Whilst it is important to point out potential dangers and threats, we should only make employees mindful of them and not stare at them for too long otherwise they will become depressed. They are a useful tool to grab their attention but we should then very quickly focus that attention on the positives, the solutions and a vision for the future they can buy in to.

Debt has become a fixture of modern life and it can be very easy to slip into a negative cycle when it comes to credit cards, overdrafts and loans. It's something that people worry about and can lose sleep over. But despite all the negativity, in some circumstances I think debt used intelligently can be your best friend, because the pain attached to the worry of debt can provide the emotional driver for long-term permanent and positive change.

Now imagine if the majority of your employees were focused on the positive, a financial life plan of their own that provided a sense of financial certainty. Having and believing in a financial life plan will build their confidence to deal with life's challenges robustly rather than letting things get on top of them. It will provide them with a sense of direction and belief. Their plan may initially be set to get them out of their current debt situation, or to eliminate their long-term cashflow worries to ensure that they always have enough money whatever happens, but then it can focus on creating wealth.

If we only focus on our problems or what we don't want in life, we create an environment that encourages the very outcome we want to avoid because we cause our RAS to work against us. If we focus on our plan, on what we want and why we want it, psychologically this vision and positive outcome becomes much bigger, much clearer and eventually overshadows our worries as we use our RAS to work for us.

It creates a new environment that improves our chances of success. Remember our personal radar is becoming more sensitive to things that will help us achieve the outcome we desire, in this case our vision for a great financial life. If we can help create a positive vision to focus on, employees' problems will appear smaller contextually and they will feel in control, especially of their emotions. We are not changing the situation, just the way they think about it, which has a positive impact on their overall wellbeing.

The primary motivators

Humans have two primary motivators, pain and pleasure[2]. Every thought and action we have is as a result of our need to avoid pain or move towards pleasure, which we have developed as part of our survival instinct. Of those two, avoidance of pain is by far the strongest. If you attach a lot of pain to something, especially if you believe it has the potential to kill you, then you want to avoid it at all costs. But while pain is a good motivator in some respects, in an extreme situation it can push people the other way - they can block it out and ignore it.

We certainly need to get people to understand the pain of not doing things like saving for their future or retirement, but we should actually spend more time and energy showing them the positives of putting plans in place. You need the experience of planning their future to be pleasurable; and as a business, you want each and every employee to form positive associations with your company and continuing to work for you. Ideally, we want employees to make good financial decisions based on moving towards pleasure rather than to avoid perceived

[2] This statement is referenced in multiple publications and research undertaken by the creators of NLP Bandler & Grinder

pain. Both work but we all prefer to do things for positive reasons.

The primary motivators are useful tools in grabbing employees' attention too especially pain. Whilst we can use pain to get their attention, such as focusing them on what they stand to lose if they don't pay attention, we must always very quickly switch to the positive emotion of moving towards pleasure.

Use the right language

Keep it simple. No jargon. If you use financial people, take care that they don't communicate in their usual financial terminology. It is important to maintain engagement, however, if an employee hears something they do not understand their brain gets stuck on it and for several minutes anything else they hear is not going in. They may miss important information. Think about reading a book. If you read a word that you do not understand, even though you carry on reading for a couple more pages it is very difficult to recall anything that has been read after the offending word, it's best to stop and grab a dictionary.

Also, choose words carefully as employees attach negative feelings to certain words. I often ask an audience to shout out words they associate with the term "pension". What I get back is: complicated, expensive, lose money, money tied up, misselling scandal; none which are positive. As a result, I tend to use the word retirement instead. If employees feel confused by jargon or focus on negative thoughts during the process the whole thing will stall and you will struggle to keep the momentum.

Good decisions are made by emotion not logic

This is by far the biggest mistake made by financial educators. I have witnessed this for decades, seeing highly intellectual people frustrated at the negative reaction to their communication. They are totally confused as to why people do not decide to do what is so obviously the most logical thing. They even stoop so low as to make derogatory comments about their client's IQ. In fact it is they who should take a long hard look in the mirror, because they lack the knowledge of how people think, decide and act.

Yes, it may appear crazy when somebody doesn't join their firm's pension when, from a logical perspective, they get tax relief and matched contributions. However, the reason that most of these non-joiners do not join is that they have made an emotional decision not to. It is not important enough to them at this moment, and that is how our minds work. They attach more pain (emotion) to paying out money each month than to the perceived pain (emotion) of a poor retirement. To keep going on and on about the logic of matching contributions and tax relief will often push people the other way.

If, however, the situation is switched, and through a great education strategy they suddenly saw a future of themselves in poverty (this painful vision creates momentum), then they designed a plan for a future of abundance (positive vision creates positive emotion), they consequently may make the good decision to save their money every month.

The perceived pain of having no money in the future, followed by the perceived pleasure of a wonderful future helps make a good decision. All of a sudden, saving is more important to them than it was before. Nothing has changed other than the way they think about it. We have used this strategy with group personal pension communication for nearly 2 decades and we have often seen employee contributions topped up to over 10% of their earnings.

This is now when the logic becomes extremely important. Once a decision is made (always emotionally), the brain searches for logic to reinforce the decision, to confirm and to maintain. If the logic cannot be found the original decision is often reversed, so logic plays an important part in financial education but must come after the emotional aspect.

This is the most invisible aspect to financial educators. They very intellectually deliver a lot of very useful technical information to employees, but it's like water off a duck's back. It doesn't permeate because it does not connect with them emotionally. Their experience can be lacklustre and the all-important office grapevine cannot do its job in promoting the financial education further.

The tools of effective communication

There are three tools used in communication: words, voice qualities and physiology. This may seem fairly obvious to many people but it is the proportion that we use each tool that is all important. There is simply too much reliance on words only, i.e. written words to deliver information.

Words only make up around 10% of our communication with one another[3] - so simply directing people to a website and expecting them firstly to read it, and secondly to engage with the content, isn't enough.

---

[3] Bandler & Grinder

A financial education website to support a well-constructed financial education programme certainly has its place, but you cannot rely on it to really make a difference. There's also the concern that if people read the information, words, in the wrong frame of mind, they misunderstand it and take a different message away from it than the one you intended. For example, a message read when stressed can have a different meaning to one read when relaxed.

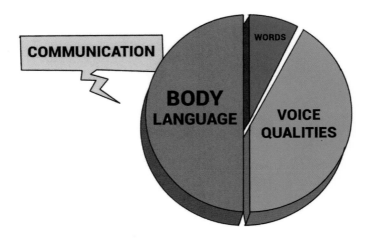

Words have much more meaning when spoken because now the voice qualities come into play. Voice qualities represent around 40% of our communication. What are voice qualities? The tempo, pitch, volume, pace, intonation and resonance all say far more than the words themselves. In fact, the way we say things is four times more powerful than what we say.

The remaining 50% is the physiology of the communicator, or educator in this instance. This is body language, posture, gestures, facial expressions and eye contact. Most of it isn't something we notice consciously, but it has a big impact on whether you trust someone, and consequently whether you take the information or message they're sharing onboard.

This unconscious aspect of communication is difficult to articulate, but it's a feeling created by the unconscious messages that come from the body language of the speaker. You know that feeling you have when you don't believe what somebody is saying but you don't have a reason, it's usually because of incongruence between the words that are being said, how they are being said and the physiology.

When you think of it in those terms, you wonder why you'd only want to use 10% of the tools available to you to when you're talking about something so fundamentally important to people's overall wellbeing. In a nutshell, always aim to use all the tools of effective communication if at all possible. It is not always possible or practical, but if you can reach a stage where all the communication is delivered by real people in the presence of your employees, it will have the best chance of succeeding.

Enhancing employee resilience

I'm incredibly passionate about the concept of financial freedom - the idea that you have enough wealth to not have to worry about money and are in control of most things financial in your life. When you have that, you feel an enormous sense of freedom, but it also helps you become more resilient.

If we can increase the resilience of employees then they will be able to tackle life's shocks better. Not just financial shocks, but personal shocks too. If they have a sense of financial freedom and certainty, then they won't have any money worries to compound whatever other problems they have. This should have a positive impact on their overall wellbeing and be good for business.

This is an incredibly powerful thing to give your employees. You want them to think of themselves as RoboCop, with bullets bouncing off their armour. Financial freedom is that armour, and will allow them to face difficult situations with confidence and come out unscathed.

Using financial education to build that resilience and robustness is really important. One of the most powerful tools I've encountered to help people visualise their future financial situation is cashflow forecasting. You can provide a cashflow forecast to anyone as a starting point - and that's really important because to achieve financial freedom you need to start with the end in mind, which for the majority of people is retirement.

In essence, what this forecast does is show you when you might run out of money, for example, so you can adjust your current strategy to prevent that from happening. In many cases, especially if you're younger, those adjustments will be quite minor.

While it's an incredibly useful tool, the idea of predicting your financial future can be quite difficult for some people who may not want to face the truth, but what we, as advocates of financial education, have to communicate is that it's better to deal with those facts and make adjustments now rather than wait for things to fall apart in the future. You need to get your employees to think of it as a compass that's guiding them through life, and while they may get knocked off course from time to time, they'll still be able to find their way back and ultimately reach their destination.

Having worked with employee benefits, including pensions, for nearly 15 years, I knew the importance of planning for the future. But it was when I moved into the private client side of the industry about five years ago that I discovered cashflow forecasting, which for me has become an invaluable tool in helping people achieve financial freedom, whatever their current status.

By blending everything I'd learned about financial planning with my years of working in employee benefits, financial education was born. My greatest epiphany was finding a way to introduce cashflow forecasting to every employee who wants it in the workplace. Initially it was considered to be a tool that was only of use to the very wealthy, but when you look closer you realise it's just about numbers and that this kind of forecast has value to everyone.

It is especially essential for those close to retirement because nowadays employees will be trying to juggle a range of income sources and flexible pension withdrawals, as well as a longer life expectancy. The stress here is running out of money too quickly. The questions they have are about which asset to spend first, how to invest in the meantime, how to look after the family, inheritance tax planning, gifting and so on. It's too much for anybody to be expected to know what to do. A good cashflow forecast can take that worry away. It can help your employees arrange their affairs so that they can aim to bounce their last cheque the day they die!

As an employer, being able to provide everyone who works for you with a great financial education has numerous benefits, from helping people stop worrying about money to giving them some clarity about their future aspirations, both personally and in terms of their career. Working through each of the four stages of a financial wellbeing strategy is empowering and once people understand the concept, it's usually something they want to do and see immense value in.

The rest of this book will look at how to deliver your broader financial education programme in four distinct stages.

2 Promoting Your Financial Education Programme

Promotion of your financial education programme is an area that is overlooked enormously and the part of the process that can cause the greatest upset. A poorly promoted financial education strategy will almost certainly fail after the initial flurry of interest. I have heard employers say that they will simply send out some emails and then they feel frustrated when their employees don't act upon them. We will explore promotion in this chapter and you will learn from the many mistakes we have made over the years to save you from the disappointment that a well-intended, but poorly attended, financial education programme can create.

What is your why?

To get off to a good start it is crucial to know why you are introducing a financial education programme, and everybody involved needs to understand the drivers and the objectives of the organisation.

When speaking with employers they often simply say that they want their employees to be more financially savvy, but this is a little too vague in my opinion. There is usually a more strategic reason if you dig a little deeper.

Common reasons why employers want a financial education programme:

- A duty of care, because pay rises have been subdued whilst the cost of living has gone up for several years slowly squeezing employees' lifestyles and potentially their wellbeing.
- You are concerned at the amount of debt issues you have witnessed, which are affecting employee attitudes and stress levels.
- Since the introduction of pensions automatic enrolment you have noticed that employee contributions to pensions are too low and you have many opt-outs.
- Since the removal of default retirement ages you are experiencing a significant number of employees working into their late 60s.
- Future workforce planning - your average employee age may have crept up and you would like to empower older employees to retire in an elegant and respectful way.
- You have used financial advisers in the past to help employees funded by pension provider commission, but this has now been removed and like many firms you cannot justify paying the necessary fees instead.
- You operate a graduate recruitment programme and have noticed that these new employees have as much as £50,000 of student debt when they start work.
- You may simply have a sense of strong paternalism and want to do the right thing by your employees (my favourite).

- You are concerned about the consequences of doing nothing.
- You have decided to introduce financial education as an employee benefit.
- You want to increase employees' financial understanding as a way of enhancing the perceived value of the employee benefits package.
- A recent legislative change has impacted on a section of your employee community and they need to know what to do about it.

Whatever your reasons, this is the place to start and this should be shared with anybody involved in helping deliver it. It always works better when all the stakeholders are aligned behind a common goal - just like any project that you may manage through the business.

Next, you need to consider your overall objectives and desired outcome. Is this to be a short-term project over three months, six months or a year? Is it a three-year plan, or is it something that you want to continually evolve? Do you want it to be run passively? I.e. it runs continuously and employees get involved as and when they wish. Or do you want a proactive strategy of targeting a certain number or percentage of employees, or do you have specific needs to deal with in a certain community at your firm?

Here is a brilliant question to ask yourself, one I have used with countless clients, to ensure you design your ideal outcome:

> "If we were sitting here one/two/three years/months from now and looking back, what has to have happened in order for you to feel happy with the progress of your financial education programme?"[4]

Answer that and you will have a much clearer picture of exactly what you want to achieve. It really draws focus to the drivers behind your programme and the true benefits to employees and the business. Once this vision is clear, a useful next step could be to do a S.W.O.T analysis of the business in relation to the financial education programme objectives. This creates a higher degree of confidence and allows you to anticipate problems and tackle them in advance. Involving everyone in its design can generate excitement, which will help the project complete.

It will also help with the creation of your project management plan. If your firm is of a reasonable size this is always a good idea to keep the

---

[4] The R-Factor Question®, Dan Sullivan and Strategic Coach. See http://blog.strategiccoach.com/dan-sullivans-r-factor-question/ and http://blog.strategiccoach.com/the-great-sales-conversation/ for more information

momentum, as is assigning a project manager if you want to ensure a successful delivery.

Take stock

Before you get started, it is wise to know where you are today. I would always recommend some form of measurement now, to take stock of your employees' financial well-being at present to allow you to draw comparisons when you have completed the various phases of the project.

It is important here not to conduct surveys that are too product or specific-topic led though, because employees do not know how to answer the questions. It is better to ask questions about how employees are feeling about their finances rather than ask what specific education they think they want. Until they become more aware of the things they should learn about, their answers are usually inaccurate.

There are some useful surveys available at only a very small cost from some reputable not-for-profit organisations. Whilst they are not for profit, they are also not for loss so expect to pay around £1 per survey. If you use a 'for profit' organisation, their surveys are usually designed to lead to a purchase of their services.

The not-for-profit organisations can provide an individual employee report which they can keep, but more importantly you can obtain the overall corporate perspective report. You won't get every employee to complete one, but you should go for as many as possible so that the results are as clear a snapshot of the financial stress within your firm as possible.

At the end of the project, it is easier to get employees who have been through the programme to complete their survey. You can then see what is and isn't working, and fine tune the process.

Grabbing employees' attention

When you introduce a financial education programme at your organisation, the first stumbling block is often making sure your employees know it exists. In the flood of internal communications that get sent out via email each week, it's easy for people to overlook something like a new financial education programme.

Ideally we need to get this project on their radar, as mentioned earlier, so that they notice it and attach a positive feeling to it. You may also need to tap into one of the primary motivators - pleasure or pain - to get people to sit up and take notice. A financial wellbeing strategy doesn't necessarily sound like the most exciting thing in the world to your busy employees. In fact if you ask them if they'd like to learn more about pensions, most will probably say no thanks! And when people are busy, opening an introductory email, let alone reading it, could easily go straight to the bottom of their to-do list.

So how can you get them to take notice? You trigger their RAS (remember from earlier in the book?). We've discovered that one of the most effective ways to do this is to write a letter to them at home.

"Really?" you say. Yes, an old fashioned way of communicating can work wonders for the introduction of a new initiative like this. Emails are no longer unique and exciting, most of us receive dozens if not hundreds of them a day. But personalised letters have become a lot less commonplace nowadays. A personalised letter signed by someone senior in the business, that introduces a new initiative will carry a lot more weight. You can almost guarantee that it will be opened by the recipient.

For a start, people will receive and open it at home, when they're away from the distractions of work and when they have more time to actually read the information you're sharing with them. It's a very powerful tool to make sure initiatives like this are on people's radars, that we've triggered their RAS.

This is the opportunity to introduce not just the benefits of the project but also the brand, if you create one, and/or the name of the project. You may link the name and brand to your employee benefits package brand if you have one, which can work very neatly.

You should also use this opportunity to involve your marketing department and consider how to make the look and feel of the project familiar to the firm's brand or that of the benefits package.

The key thing is that once they have read their letter, they will be more likely to notice, open and read any follow-up email about your financial wellbeing strategy, because they're now familiar with the concept, the brand and the name.

Treat the promotion like any other marketing campaign you execute

Communication and sending out the right messages at these early stages is incredibly important. To get the maximum positive impact from your correspondence with employees, consider again tapping into the expertise of your marketing department. They will have the tools, knowledge and skills to firstly get your message out to people, and to secondly craft those messages to engage people from the start.

You should treat it as a marketing campaign in its own right; a campaign to raise awareness of financial wellbeing among your workforce and help them achieve that all important financial freedom. When you think of it in those terms, involving your marketing department is suddenly obvious. You can use their CRM system to access relevant employee data and start looking at segmenting your audience so that you can send targeted messages to different groups of people.

For example, we've found that the most difficult group to get involved are the high earners. You need to use something strong to get their attention - and the most effective way is to tap into their 'pain' motivator by making them understand they could lose out by not getting involved. They won't pay attention if they're not emotionally charged about losing something; this has to be more important than their short-term work responsibilities. Once you've got their attention, you can educate them about how to solve their problem.

An example of what can work for high earners is that the tax rules around pensions seem to change each year and recent rule changes have been very complex and difficult to understand. Many high earners are going to get a nasty surprise when they complete their tax returns and find they have an unexpected tax bill. Using this information you can craft a simple but emotive message to grab their attention and then drive them towards the solution through the education programme. This is their primary motivator of 'avoiding pain' at work.

But this may not be the most effective way of reaching out to other groups of staff. This is why targeting and careful marketing is so important. Your communication needs to be spot on from the start to avoid losing people because they don't think what you're telling them is relevant to their lives.

Inspect what you expect

Once your campaign is underway, you can use the CRM system to monitor who's receiving what emails, how many people are opening them and who is clicking through to register for events about your financial wellbeing programme. This marketing insight is extremely useful as it allows you to refine your approach and try again.

It will also allow you to pinpoint any groups of employees who seem disengaged. You can investigate why they aren't engaging, run some targeted marketing to get them involved, and really focus on selling the benefits of a financial wellbeing strategy to their lives.

Monitoring will also allow you to do several more logistical things. You can effectively plan your events to ensure there is adequate space for everyone who wants to attend. If you're targeting 40 people for an event due to room size but see that subscription is up to 80, you can move your event to a larger room. Or you can set up additional events to cater for the demand without losing the momentum of your campaign.

Timing and frequency

There can be a number of reasons why people aren't engaging with financial education. As an example, we were working with a business that had terrible attendance at its financial education events from one particular office.

When we looked more closely, we discovered that this office was predominantly made up of salespeople and that the events we'd been running were falling in the final two to three weeks of their quarter, when their focus is on their quota and thus their bonus. This was always going to be more important to them in the short term. By simply moving events to the first week or two after a sales quarter cut-off date, we saw attendance increase to normal levels, because they had time to relax and think about other things before focusing on the next quarter's targets.

This shows the value of segmenting your audience and targeting your efforts at different groups of employees, particularly in a large organisation.

One thing we have also learned here is that the frequency of the email communication itself is crucial. If you send out too many vague email invitations too regularly, employees stop noticing them and in fact delete them as soon as they arrive. The campaign can easily go stale. You do have to work at it to get the result you require, think of the programme as a marathon not a sprint, but the emails must not become a pest. Do not send out invitations more than twice per week or you lose the RAS that you triggered early on. The RAS works against you as it now does its job of filtering out what it believes the employee does not need to notice right this minute!

If you send an email one week on a Monday morning, try sending on a Tuesday afternoon the following week. This will help increase the opens by a wider audience who may have differing email reading patterns.

Email templates

To maximise the open, read and click-through rate of these emails they require some thought to ensure the messaging is strong. The way emails are structured is often overlooked. Too many times I have I heard people say, "Just send an email", only to get a really poor response. Remember the objective here is to get your targeted community to read and act on these emails. It is crucial to take some time to craft them carefully and with the help of your marketing department.

The subject line should feel very personal, written in the second person so that the focus is on the recipient. It should ideally contain the word you, your or yours. This increases the open rate.

The subject line also works better when there is the offer of a change to the status quo e.g. "How effective is your retirement planning?" or "Could you be getting more from your money?" The subject line is crucial because some emails are set up to be seen in the viewing pane next to the email list even before it is opened. If the subject line doesn't grab their attention at this stage it could be deleted before it is opened.

The content of the email should align with the subject line otherwise the reader feels tricked into opening it and this can increase unsubscribes. It should have a simple, punchy message that teases the content and an easy to spot 'register now' button. Also, as such a large proportion of emails are read on mobile devices, make sure the email body is mobile optimised.

If you design specific subject lines for specific employees then there is little point sending the email to those who would be unlikely to relate to it. Therefore, this is an opportunity to segment and target the messaging more strategically so employees receive fewer emails, keeping the campaign fresher for longer. You could segment in the following ways:

- Young adults
- Middle-aged employees
- Those nearing retirement
- Parents
- Offsite/homeworkers
- High earners or senior employees
- Different locations
- Those specifically affected by some recent legislative change
- New employees.

By considering the specific situations of various employee segments like this you can avoid the blanket email approach which so often misses the mark. You know your employees best, so work with your marketing department and craft your campaign to suit.

Employee endorsements

Once your programme has commenced you should always be obtaining feedback from the participants (more on this in Chapter 3). If you gather employee comments and their permission to use them they can be added to future email invitations. We usually look for three strong comments and work them into the body of the email with the employee name and job title. If they are a well-known employee this works even better. Why three? People love threes; three is small enough to read but big enough to have credibility.

Also, you can change the email subject line to something like: 'See what your colleagues have been saying' or 'Three reasons why you do not want to miss out' - you can be as creative as you like here.

Don't rely on just the written word

Remember, communication is more than just words; words represent just 10% of how we communicate. So while letters and written emails have a purpose, so too do other communication methods. For instance, putting together a short video to explain the main messages can be highly effective as it's something different, and it isn't necessarily difficult or costly to make.

Try stitching together a video, no longer than three minutes, of a senior person, a well-known sceptical employee and maybe the lead of the project making an impassioned plea to get employees to register and attend the events. This way you use all the tools of communication: words, voice and body language. A well-known sceptic is also a clever tool, because other employees think that if he/she is sufficiently impressed then it must be worthwhile!

The professionalism and picture quality of the video is not so important in these days of video blogging, YouTube pages and video messaging. What is important is the sound quality. In fact, a very basic background with no special effects can feel more personal with the focus being on the message and not the production. However, the sound needs to be good, because people will switch off very quickly if they struggle to hear.

We have even used a smartphone and selfie stick to record some basic video messaging, but we did invest in a directional microphone. They cost very little from any decent computer shop, but the way they avoid background noise is quite amazing for something so low cost. With this in mind, there is no excuse for you not to mix up the style of messaging. Don't think about it too long, just record the message, check the sound, host the video somewhere and then email out a simple link to the video.

Always have a camera/smartphone (with that all-important directional microphone) available at the events you run and if anyone is particularly motivated about what they've learned, make sure you film their reaction and get their permission to use it to promote your financial education programme to other employees.

Alternative video

There are plenty of ways of cheaply and effectively creating a video where words appear on screen while the content is read over the top, they even provide some background music. Despite being low cost, these look high quality and expensive, setting the right tone for your financial education programme. There are various solutions on the internet - you could try the site Fiverr.com. I recently created a really cool promotional video message in exactly this way in just 15 minutes from start to finish. So there is no excuse to avoid getting creative!

Create an animation

Another creative way to spice things up is to use animation. You may find that your marketing department has the tools and talent to create this for you. As employees are all different and learn in different ways this may be the way to get the attention of a few. It can also help prevent all your emails looking too similar.

Like video, it needs to be short, maybe even shorter as the human face is not involved. If you do not possess the resources or people internally to create your short animation there are plenty of solutions. There is software for this type of thing, but if you do not want to purchase any or learn how to do it you can buy a short animation very cost effectively. There are lots of very bright people who can create your animation for you from their bedrooms, and they charge only a few pounds. You can also find them on Fiverr.com. So there is no excuse not to be creative here either.

Word of mouth is your most powerful tool

Don't underestimate the value of having advocates within your workforce who can help sell the value of financial wellbeing to other employees. Testimonials and endorsements are incredibly powerful, especially if they come from someone trusted by their colleagues, or someone at work who's renowned for being cynical. One of the best ways to capture these is on video as mentioned earlier. Simply having people within your workforce who have engaged with the process and fully appreciate the benefits will help your financial wellbeing strategy gain traction.

Generating that excitement and engagement can sometimes be a challenge though, as can rolling out a scheme to the entire workforce. Starting with a pilot scheme is a good option, especially for large organisations.

This allows you to test the water with a select group of employees and by getting them to buy into the process, you'll have strong advocates within your workforce who will help other employees get involved once it's rolled out more widely. You need to manage expectations carefully with those involved, to make sure they understand that you're running it as a pilot, but if you can get influential people on board at this stage it can really help with your promotion of financial education if you expand that to the rest of your workforce.

Registration and attendance

If you are using a CRM system you can automate registrations. This is crucial, as to attempt this manually will seriously get out of control with people not knowing where they are going, and this can mean negativity about the project can creep in and kill it. This negativity is not about the quality of the content; it's about the way the disorganisation makes people feel.

You can set up financial education events and count as employees register because you will have to remove the events that fill up. Due to attendance rates rarely being 100%, you can always allow a little oversubscription of around 25%. In our experience, the registrations and attendance are high at the beginning so we wouldn't oversubscribe for the first few events, but after that it's fine.

Even if you do have too many employees turn up at an event, it is actually quite interesting to see the motivation and excitement it creates. They rush to grab a chair or go looking for chairs to drag in and sit at the back. This is actually a great experience to get the mood of the room set up at the start (more about this later).

Once an employee has registered for an event, they should receive two things: an email confirmation and an electronic calendar invitation. Depending on the type of business you are, this may not be feasible but if possible it is a must. You want them to accept the event into their calendar now.

Not all CRM systems offer a calendar invite option, however, that is no excuse because you can easily and cheaply find them on the internet. These need to be hard wired into the confirmation email and placed into calendars. Your attendance rates will plummet if you don't, because a significant number of employees do not get round to placing the event into their calendar manually and all too often something else is entered that clashes.

Ideally, you will also set up automated email reminders. An email reminder the day before is useful and also a chaser 15 minutes before the event is crucial. If employees only remember at the last minute they will often not turn up out of the embarrassment of walking in late. If you have a sophisticated CRM system you can send a phone text reminder, as people will nearly always read a text but not always read an email.

Financial education website or intranet

This is not always practical or possible, but if you can set this up it is a great way to help with the promotion and administration of the programme. Either a bespoke website or presence on your intranet can support your endeavour. Some firms have their employee benefits package information hosted online and it can help in the following ways:

- Providing a go-to place for information about the programme.
- Hosting updated information for employees to revisit regularly.
- Acting as a technical information resource. We would recommend that the detail is kept to a high level with hyperlinks to downloadable fact sheets for those who want all the detail.
- Be a hub for other downloadable content such as financial updates, budget summaries and legislation changes.
- Messaging can also be delivered by video to compliment the written word for all the reasons stated in Chapter 1.
- Events calendar centralised management, as these change constantly.
- Providing a description of the content and benefits of each financial education event.

- Sharing contact details of the events coordinator and helpline if available.
- A link to the events registration page.
- Signposting to various employee solutions within the employee benefits package or the financial education programme - you can add pages to explain the employee benefits package.

Management buy-in

The all-important line manager is a great resource to help encourage employees to get involved. They see the commercial benefits to the business of employees feeling financially well, and they also have a personal relationship with their team which will usually mean that they care about their welfare. If they buy in on both counts they can be your greatest advocate.

Look for opportunities to engage with this important group. Can you start the programme with this group so that they can champion it to the other employees? Do they ever meet as a group giving you the opportunity to communicate the programme to them? Could you get them involved on a personal basis where they see the value for themselves and then become active promoters and encourage their employees to invest some time in their financial education? This is also a great time for these managers to notice any employee stress that they may have missed; an opportunity for them to help steer employees that they suspect may be struggling to move towards some of the solutions available through the programme.

Beware though that not all managers will buy in straight away, especially the sales teams if they are pushing for deadlines and year-end bonuses. You may have to pick your moment!

In A Nutshell

The promotion of your programme requires perseverance but without becoming a pest. It is a fine balance between keeping it front of mind and making it stale. Try different things, inspect the results and refine accordingly. All workforces are different and you know your people.

3 Creating Awareness For Optimum Results

Employees need to know what they need to know

We have learned that we need to really help employees to 'know what it is they need to know about'. Don't assume they already know, if you leave it to them to decide without making them aware of a much wider perspective they may choose to do nothing or choose to learn about something that is not the most important or relevant topic to them and their families right now. If your employees have to think too much their motivation will fizzle out.

Imagine promoting an estate planning educational tutorial to your workforce right now. What interest would you expect there to be? Pretty low I would imagine. We have learned that this particular topic is actually the second most popular among employees. In some firms it is number one! Why you might say? We have learned (the hard way!) that we have to make employees aware of the importance of learning about certain subjects before we offer them the education on those subjects.

They need to see, in simple terms, the concept and the potential impact, good and bad, to them and their families. We must put the topic into the context of their lives, avoid using features or technical language and focus on the benefits. Once this is done they can then make an informed choice about what they need to learn about. We have found that without this stage of 'awareness' it is very difficult to get the right people to learn about the most appropriate topics at the right time.

The awareness presentation

Think of this presentation as the employees' introduction to the rest of the education programme. It is the part that 'sells' its value to employees and creates a great deal of appreciation that as an employer you are offering such a valuable employee benefit. Its purpose is to do three important things:

1. To introduce employees to the value of the programme to them
2. To inform them of the next stages of more specific education
3. To enable them to self-select, in an informed way, which topics they need and want educating on at the next stage.

This stage actually becomes part of the promotion process in that it helps you get the right people to the relevant topics. Through our own bitter experience we have learned that a programme can succeed or fail at this stage. It sets the tone for the rest of the programme so it's where your best presenters should be deployed and they should be prepared and on top form for the benefit of the employees.

The structure of the presentation, whether it is delivered face to face or via webcast, should be highly graphic and simple. Remember, a picture paints a thousand words. AVOID BULLET POINTS AT ALL TIMES!! Again, we'll go into detail on this when we cover presenting.

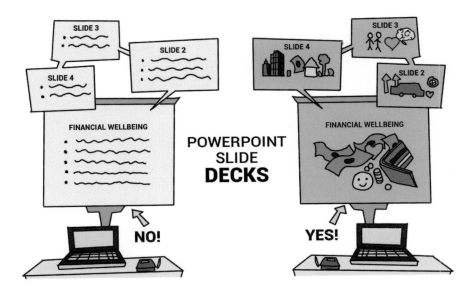

Each slide should be up for no more than about a minute. It should contain a basic image or animation that helps the presenter explain the subject but does not explain it on its own. The presenter needs to fully understand the meaning of the slide and use the imagery to help deliver the message, but the slide itself without a presenter should be meaningless.

This way the presenter is forced to communicate at a deeper level, and in a more natural way, with the audience. It takes the pressure to deliver scripted content away and leaves it to the presenter to naturally convey meaning. The presenter controls the presentation not the other way around. When a presenter isn't in control it can feel very unnatural and the audience slowly disconnects and their minds wander.

After the presentation, most people usually forget much of the detail and content, but they rarely forget the way it made them feel. This is the stage where your internal grapevine is born and it will be a very positive one if the attendees have enjoyed the experience.

The other thing you need to overcome is the fact that you're talking about finances, which most people will expect to be dry and maybe a little dull before you even start. When they have enjoyed and been inspired by the presentation, this contrast to their initial expectation can play a large part in their enthusiasm towards the programme going forward and is very welcome feedback to the HR team who are usually the ones who facilitated it. There is usually a little apprehension from the project sponsors at the beginning, so a great kick off with a very strong initial introductory presentation provides much comfort and relief.

How to make a presentation memorable

Isn't this the whole point? A presentation or tutorial needs to achieve 3 things, it needs to be impressive, engaging and most importantly, memorable. Once you understand this next bit, you will never look at a presentation in the same way again! Around 90% of presentations are made up of slides that have a title and a list of bullet points. A bad presenter just reads out bullet points, a worse presenter reads them out one at a time and then spends 3 minutes explaining the meaning of each bullet point. This just makes the presentation longer and more boring. In a vain attempt to make a presentation more attractive, some presenters even insert some clipart or a photograph.

The problem with bullet points is that you cannot process the imagery of the written bullet point and the sound of words being spoken at the same time. We process information differently if it is sound than if it is vision. When you give text in the form of a bullet point you process it phonetically, the voice inside our head reading it, then you process it the same as the sound that you hear. Then you hear it from the presenter at the same time so there are 2 voices going on!

Therefore, the simple rule is — if possible, always replace a bullet with a diagram or picture. A diagram or picture that is simple to look at but doesn't totally explain the message without the narrative of the presenter, creates the experience we need to make the presentation effective. It is called visual cognitive dissonance (Google it!). This is another of those things that are completely invisible to most financial educators.

It's visual because the audience is looking at it, cognitive because the audience is thinking about it and dissonance because it is not obvious what they are looking at. Their internal voice is asking "What is that?" They then focus on the presenter to tell them the answer. The curiosity that is created makes the audience pay much more attention, they lean forward and they listen intently waiting for an explanation or to see what the next click of the animation will bring.

Research conducted by the University of Central Lancashire in this area highlighted that people only remember 1 or 2 out of 5 bullet points, however, 95% can accurately remember a diagram or an image. The research also highlighted that 85% of the non-visual content, the narrative around the slides, is also remembered. Basically, because they pay more attention and are more engaged, they remember more. Isn't that what presentations are about?

Also, using animation to build a slide in steps works well because if there is a lot of empty space on a slide at the beginning, it is obvious to the audience that it will be filled with content very soon. It sort of creates a story that the audience want to get to the end of, i.e. they are paying attention.

In a nutshell, your return on investment and time will suffer if you use bullet points. Remove as much text as possible and replace with diagrams and pictures. Then aim to animate with a narrative over the top and your presentations will become more engaging, more memorable and ultimately more effective.

Preparation prevents p*** poor performance

Simple advice: presenters should not create unnecessary pressure for themselves by getting off to a bad start. Get to the venue early, set up the presentation, test the animation, projection and sound if applicable. Make sure seating is set up correctly, minimise seats at the back, put handouts on chairs, registration and pens at the ready. Take a deep breath and then relax. If any of this is rushed and last minute it will put the presenter under pressure which will affect the unconscious communication.

This is vital, because if an audience feels the presenter is nervous they can easily assume it is because of a lack of belief rather than a lack of preparation. This will fuel heckling and put the presenter under even more pressure, often killing the value and setting off a negative grapevine.

The presenter should also carry a spare battery for a presentation remote control (always use one of these!) and always carry a copy of the presentation on a memory stick in case of a computer malfunction. It is the presenter's responsibility to deliver the highest quality experience to attendees. If the presenter messes up, he or she will live to fight another day. However, the attendees could walk away with a poor experience which may influence them the wrong way with their finances - a terrible outcome.

Educators need to have passion for the subject

If you're going to run a financial education programme that has real benefits to your employees, every presenter or web caster has to be passionate about their subject. They need to approach each session with the attitude of how many people can I help in the next 45 minutes? They need to have a sense of responsibility when delivering a session, transferring their belief and conviction to every attendee to ensure the best and most appropriate outcome for everyone who's there.

Presenters need to understand their responsibility and embrace it. They need to be well-rehearsed, energised and compelling in every session. You should make sure you only use professionally trained, tried and tested presenters to deliver a financial education programme. You want to be able to promote them as experts, but remember that they are also the face of your programme - they're your ambassador and it's imperative that employees not only like and trust them, but also enjoy the process and benefit from it.

Creating that buzz and excitement will do more for a programme and employee morale than internal comms and a website ever will. You want your employees to be actively promoting the programme to others who are cynical of it through the internal grape-vine, and because you've provided them with a wealth of information in your sessions, they can be incredibly influential over those who are cynical but don't have the information to back up their opinions.

We've discovered that a well-run financial education programme can be your most successful employee engagement initiative.

Positive focus

As well as relevancy, the other thing you need to be really mindful of is focus, and where you focus people's minds. We're talking about financial wellness and financial wellbeing, which is the opposite of financial stress and anxiety. While you sometimes need to use those pain triggers to elicit a response, you don't want to keep people in a state of fear.

And you need to remember that a lot of the financial anxiety people carry around actually isn't real. It's something they've focused on and worried about in their heads, but that doesn't necessarily reflect reality. The concern is that if you focus too much on the negative then you encourage those negative tendencies in real life.

So, for instance, if someone focuses their thoughts on, 'I don't want to be in debt', then what they're actually doing is generating fear around the idea of debt. In most cases, that increases their likelihood of getting into, or staying in, debt. What they actually need to do is focus on abundance and having a great life. While they still need to be mindful of debt, they shouldn't make that the focus.

Shifting from a negative to a positive perspective will be incredibly motivating. Working towards what you want gives you something to aim for. If we try not to think about something, we have to make a mental image of it before we then try to not think about it! If I say to you, "Don't think about a blue tree", what are you thinking about? See? So it's crucial that we take care in where we focus employees' minds.

Let's be mindful of the negative, but then let's spend the majority of our time on the positives and solutions. What we have to do, as financial educators, is get employees to stop focusing on what they don't want and start focusing on what they do want, shift the focus to financial wellbeing, rather than financial anxiety.

Personalise every presentation

The presenter should start by greeting each and every person as they come into the room. The same goes for webcasts. Check their names off a register that you have pulled from your CRM database and registration system. Even if you're presenting to a room of 100 people, you should try your best to form a personal connection and bond with every person.

The presenter should aim to say hello and use the first name of each person as they enter, not always possible, but a great aim nonetheless. Each individual's name is the most precious word in their vocabulary. Say it, and a bond is formed. They feel connected to the experience, especially if you can remember it and say it again later.

Laughter

Laughter is scientifically proven to be good for your health. It has positive effects on physical, mental and social wellbeing. When laughing, neurotransmitters in our brains called dopamines are fired off which help with motivation and focus - useful in the workplace! There are many ways of increasing dopamine levels, such as exercise, nutrition, meditation and music. But the easiest and fastest way is through laughter. If the presenter can get the audience laughing early on the tone is set and they are more receptive and cooperative.

When you stand up to start your presentation, try to bring a bit of humour to the room. As I've said, most people will have pretty low expectations, so using a joke to make them smile, or a funny story to capture their attention at the beginning, makes the job of presenting easier as the audience are involved and energised. They also 'anchor' the good feelings of laughter to the programme and are more compelled to promote this experience to others.

Presenters should have a few jokes up their sleeve, or at least a unique way of breaking the ice and relaxing people into the presentation. Nothing crude, but something topical or current will usually work.

Be a storyteller

Stories are such a powerful way of educating people because they can relate to them. Presenters should have a bunch of stories up their sleeve for their presentations. The pressure is off and you can feel the engagement in the room when the presenter is telling a story to make a point or teach a lesson.

Often when you notice a presenter may appear a little nervous at the beginning of a session, you can actually feel the mood in the room change when he/she tells their story. Their delivery slows down, they relax and they do not focus on their 'script'. Their communication becomes much more congruent and flowing. The more stories the better, as long as they are relevant and even better if they are funny. As mentioned earlier, you can sort of create a story that is a sequence of events or information delivered in steps by way of animation on your slides.

Stories put the audience into a bit of a trance as they create their own images of the story in their minds, and they enable you to keep the momentum going for longer because the audience is keen to get to the end of the story. Most people can only manage to focus on live delivered content for about 25 minutes, I have seen stories told to an audience for two to three hours and they have maintained their focus the whole time. Never underestimate the power of a good and funny story.

Pace yourself

There's a lot of information to include at this stage and not all of the information you have to talk about will be relevant to everyone in that room at that very moment in their lives. The pace of the presenter is crucial, to give those it is relevant to enough information to put that subject on their radar but at the same time without the rest of the audience switching off.

With that in mind, make sure you're not talking about a particular subject for more than five minutes. Most people can live with five minutes of information that's irrelevant to them provided it's delivered in an engaging way and that the majority of the rest of the information is useful.

Interact

Interact with your audience by asking rhetorical and interactive questions to bring otherwise dry financial information to life. If you are often throwing out a question to the audience they feel they need to listen just in case the presenter picks them out for an answer. A group 'show of hands' keeps the energy high too.

Also, less is more. It is useful to understand the power of a pause. Give people time to digest the important information you're giving them. Ask a question, and then wait for an answer, presenters have to be brave here as there's a temptation to keep some sort of noise going, but continually talking is a sign of nervousness.

Props can help

An example that particularly stuck with me was when I was presenting about Wills and estate planning. On that day, I just happened to have a copy of my own Will with me. So I took it out, showed it to the audience and asked them if they knew what it was. Someone replied, 'It's your Will'. My response was measured. I said, 'It's not just my Will,' paused to thumb through it and continued, 'It's my children's future taken care of'. After that session, we got a lot of strong feedback on estate planning. It's about making these financial concepts into something real that people can connect with.

Always leave people in the positive

You also need to make sure that any negative associations you introduce are countered by solutions and reassurance. If you're talking about debt, for example, make sure everyone understands that there's a way out, and that you're going to give them what they need to become debt free. Wherever you leave them emotionally at the end of a presentation is the feeling they will most remember.

Handouts

Another way to interact is by giving attendees something tangible to hold and take away with them. A summary sheet of your presentation is ideal, with the top points covered and some of the visual cues from your slides included to help trigger their memory when they're talking about it later with colleagues or family.

You should also consider that some of the subjects you're covering can be sensitive. People don't like to publicly admit they've got issues with debt, for instance, so providing a leaflet about the employee assistance programme - if there is one - is a nice touch to give anyone who's worried by what they've heard an impartial person to speak to. It comes back to balancing any negative feelings you invoke with positive associations and solutions.

Keep it simple

It is easy for a presenter, especially a financial services presenter, to slip into jargon and confuse people. Presenters must appreciate that the audience live in a different world and too much jargon will create a poor experience. People are often too shy to ask a presenter if they did not understand something. What happens then is their mind switches away from the presenter for a few minutes while they search for a meaning to the confusing statement or terminology.

Avoid this at all times in presentations. Keep it simple. Do not confuse or you will lose people. If in doubt, practice on a friendly audience and ask for feedback to test the presentation experience.

Getting feedback

Feedback is essential if you're going to continue to improve the presentations. Positive comments can be used to promote future events and constructive critique helps you evolve the presentation to be better each time.

The other very important purpose of the feedback form is to obtain what self-selected topics each individual wishes to learn about at the next stage. We have learned that it works much better if this is not left completely to the end, because if you take that approach attendees spend several minutes reading and completing their feedback forms and this creates a dead spot right at the end of the session. It is best to avoid this quiet, awkward feeling as it might be the last one they remember.

We have learned that the best way to get the feedback forms completed and returned quickly is to do them throughout the presentation. This also mixes up the presentation a little, makes it a little more involved and the employees get to self-select their topics as soon as they have learned about them, so you're capturing them at the right moment when they're closest to a subject and have the greatest understanding of it.

As they arrive give attendees their feedback forms, have a supply of spare pens, and whilst they wait for the others to arrive ask them to register and fill in their name and details. This gives the presenter a good excuse to talk to each attendee and to use their first name. If the number of people gets too large to do this, ask one or two of the earlier arrivals to tell the later arrivals what to do. This stimulates a really strong sense of connection with everybody in the room.

When each topic has been mentioned, direct everyone to their feedback form, where they tick the box to say yes or no to further education on that particular topic, and then continue onto the next areas. This means that the form is almost completed by the end of the session, so they only have to spend maybe 30 seconds completing the last bit, avoiding the awkward silence.

Segmentation perfection

It makes a lot of sense to segment your workforce so that the financial education is delivered to the right employees at the right time. There are 2 ways to do it; either you as an employer try and segment based on the demographics of the employees, or you set up a much more accurate and meaningful employee self-segmentation arrangement. If you want absolute certainty that your financial education programme is truly effective and strategic you should let the employees self-select the topics they want education on for themselves. However, they do need to understand what topics are important and how to think about them, hence the awareness presentation. An employer can never really know and get the segmentation exactly accurate, so why even attempt it? Let the employees decide what's relevant.

Self-selection of relevant topics is absolutely crucial to keep employee appreciation high and to make sure that whatever investment you as an employer have made, that you're maximising your return. Let the employees segment themselves when they go through the initial awareness presentation and then at various stages further on in the process, and you will achieve segmentation perfection.

The right information educated to the right employees at the right time for them. Never assume you know what they want to learn about, it can appear condescending or patronising. Tell them everything available and let them choose; you will be surprised at what topics people want to learn about.

The next stage of the education needs to go deeper into detail which is fine and the attendees are able to cope and stay engaged at this deeper level because the topic is very relevant to their lives.

Our most regular surprise is when the youngest of employees arrive at an estate planning/wills educational tutorial. We asked some of them why they were attending, surely they won't have built up much of an estate yet? They stated that they have student debt and no deposit for a house. As a result they wanted to learn more details so that they could have a respectful and elegant way of broaching the subject with their parents who do have an estate; one that could be eroded through a change in family dynamics and taxes without some careful planning. The message we learned here was to never assume.

Measuring your employees' experiences with NPS

As well as finding out what's relevant, you should also be measuring the experience of financial education itself. NPS is a net promoter score and it's a very effective way of measuring customer experience. In essence, it's a simple question: How likely would you be to recommend this experience to other people you work with? People give a value between 1 and 10, 10 being extremely likely and 1 being not at all. What you're looking for is an NPS of 9s and 10s, because those people will be your active promoters. They'll help create a buzz around your programme internally and will encourage other people to get involved, boosting employee engagement.

Then you have people scoring 7s and 8s. They're what we call passively satisfied - so they're happy but they're not going to shout about it, they won't promote it.

How to get your NPS:

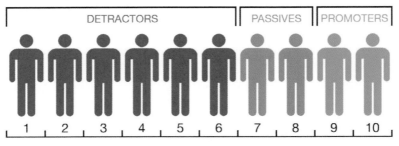

Promoters – Detractors = NPS

Typically, employees we work with score their **experience +51**.

And anyone who scores 1s to 6s would be called a detractor. They're essentially people who weren't happy with the process and you need to really watch out for these low scores, because it's these people who can spread negative word of mouth and impede the success of a financial education programme.

So when you're going through your feedback, you need to identify those and jump on them quickly. It might be that you just get one person in a session that has scored you below 7, in which case it's usually to do with them and their state of mind rather than the quality of your presentation or the information you provided. But even so, it's important to have a conversation with them, understand why they scored you that way and try to convince them that you're adding value, because even if it's not valid, their negative comments could still impact someone who hasn't yet engaged with the process.

To get your overall NPS, you take the number of 9s and 10s you scored and calculate that as a percentage of the whole group, and then you take the 1s to 6s and calculate those as a percentage - you ignore the 7s and 8s. Once you've got both percentages, you subtract the detractors' percentage from the active promoters' percentage and that's your score.

It'll be out of 100, and you'd be looking for a minimum of 30+, but any positive number shows you're going in the right direction. The key with using NPS is to measure every stage of your financial education programme individually, so that you can quickly identify any weak links in the process and correct them.

If you use well-trained and knowledgeable presenters, as covered in Chapter 2, you should easily get scores of 50+ for webcasts and presentations. When you get into one-on-one sessions, those scores usually go through the roof because people really value that experience. But you should also be measuring the tutorials, advice meetings, registration, administration and the friendliness of the human contact to get an accurate overall picture.

To give you an example of how useful NPS can be, we used them when we were developing our webcast experience. Initially, they weren't scoring as highly as the face-to-face presentations, so we got detailed feedback on each stage, tested it and made changes until the scores we were receiving for our webcasts were the same as the ones we were getting from presentations being delivered face-to-face.

Webcast presentations

Presenting in person isn't always possible, especially with the growing number of companies who employ homeworkers, so you need to be just as comfortable delivering a webcast as you do a presentation. But while the information you're covering may be the same, there are some other things you need to think about. A webcast is the next best thing to a face-to-face presentation, but the presenter has to work a little harder and pressure can be higher due to the added complexity of the technology.

When you're delivering a webcast, you need to have confidence in your technology; your webcam, computer, internet connection and microphone. Practice delivering your webcast to get used to the technology, and if you're really nervous get someone with technical expertise to sit in the room with you while you do the first couple.

The most important thing is to make sure the sound works and is clear. People can for-give a slightly blurry video feed, but if the audio goes you'll lose their attention. Always test in advance and get somebody to present to you, so you can experience and feel what the audience will when you do it.

Make it personal

In terms of delivering your presentation, you need to change your style and make each person on the webcast feel as though you're talking to them individually. Look straight at the camera, keep it natural and keep it personal. Talk to them as if they are the only person you are talking to.

As people are joining the webcast, greet them by name. Before you mute them to begin the presentation, ask them to confirm they can hear and see you ok. Respond to people, using their name. So, "Steve's in and can hear me, what about Katie? Yep, good you're there", and so on. Tell them to grab a cup of tea, a pen and a notepad. This is just small talk to make them feel like it's you and them alone and it is all very relaxed.

Think about where you are when you run your webcast as well. Your aim is to make people feel comfortable and relaxed. A professional studio environment in the office might sound great, but when you're talking to a group of people who all work from home, it can also be a bit intimidating. Running a webcast from your home will help them relax and it will feel more natural. It all comes back to building that trusting relationship with your audience.

Be prepared

You also need to check that everyone has the handouts for the meeting. Email the summary sheet, the feedback form and anything else they'll need before the webcast. Usually around 15 minutes before it's due to start is a good time to send the email, and it can be a gentle reminder that they need to join you online too.

When they join the webcast, ask them to open the handouts they need, as well as the feedback survey, so that everything is ready on-screen for when they need it.

In terms of the actual presentation, it will be pretty much the same as what you'd do live. You build the feedback into it at exactly the same points, but the advantage to webcasts is that you can get them to fill this in electronically, which means your administration after the presentation will be a lot easier and you can see all the feedback and scores within minutes of finishing.

When it comes to the final bit of feedback at the end, people find it easier to disengage and miss out that last step when they're watching online. So make a clear plea for them all to spend just 30 seconds completing that last section of the form. It might sound a bit silly but it works.

Group webcasts - a different dynamic

Group webcasts - where a group of people all watch the webcast from the same room - come with their own challenges. As with a standard webcast, technology is the big thing to test.

Make sure you have a responsible person who will be at the location so that you can run a test call and make sure the audio is loud and clear enough, and that the video works as it should. You'll also need this person to deal with the admin of handouts and feedback forms. They will need to print copies in advance to give out to everyone attending as they arrive. And they'll need to be responsible for collecting those feedback forms at the end.

During the presentation itself, people are more likely to get distracted because you aren't physically in the room with them. Before you start your presentation, ask everyone to switch their phones off, and explain the importance of the information you're about to share. You need them to give you their full attention and to understand that they will lose out if they don't.

What's wrong with a webinar?

You lose that all important sight of the face of the presenter. The audience feels a stronger connection when the presenter's face is looking directly at them, eye to eye. A webinar loses that personal touch, and people drop out sooner because they do not feel the connection.

This story explains the power of the face in communication: I want to take you back to 1960s America, the first time a US presidential debate had been televised. Nixon and JFK were the two candidates. Because TV was still relatively new at this point, there were a lot of people who were listening on radio rather than watching on TV. At the time, Nixon was slightly ahead in the approval ratings. When the polls came out after the debate, people who had only listened still put Nixon ahead, he sounded calm, his voice didn't waver and he didn't stutter.

But the people who had watched it on TV put JFK significantly ahead, because what the people listening didn't know (and couldn't see) was that Nixon was flummoxed, he was sweating a lot and he looked nervous. JFK, on the other hand, looked calm and relaxed. This TV debate, which allowed people to see the whole picture, is cited as one of the things that made the biggest difference to the JFK campaign, because of the positive associations people made with his appearance compared to Nixon's. That is a great example of why showing your face, allowing people to see you while you're talking, is so important if you want them to connect with you on an emotional level and trust what you're telling them.

4 The Power Of Education

The most important and popular financial tool

In an ideal world every employee would have a comprehensive plan for their financial lives. A plan that allows them to see the future and anticipate early any problems they are heading for. A plan that contains their goals and dreams for the future clearly mapped out with graphic simplicity. This is possible, not always easy, but definitely possible.

With a financial life plan it is much easier for employees to decide what their most important next step should be in their financial lives. It can provide a framework for the future to ensure that they are prepared for any eventuality. You could say that this is utopia and will probably never be achieved, but just imagine if a significant number of your employees, or even the majority of them, had their own plan that guided them through life and took their uncertainty away.

It would go a long way to eliminating the things they fear that stress them into a poor state of wellbeing. A plan can create that sense of financial freedom that we crave before we actually get to the stage where our assets give us that sense of financial freedom in reality, by making us feel in control of most things financial.

This is achievable and is a great place to start a financial education programme. The concept here is lifetime cashflow forecasting. This is a tool that any decent financial adviser uses with wealthy clients to ensure they optimise all of their assets, live the highest standard of life possible with what they have and never run out of money, but also don't have too much left over!

This kind of tool is extremely useful for anyone, not just wealthy people. It can provide a graphic illustration of an employee's financial future based on their current strategy and it can comp are this to their ideal outcome. They can see shortcomings now rather than when it is too late.

In psychology there are six basic human needs: love & connection, contribution, variety, growth, significance and certainty. If an individual scores themselves low in any three or more of these areas, they are highly likely to be depressed and have a poor wellbeing. If an employee is low on three areas and one happens to be certainty due their financial uncertainty, a financial life plan using lifetime cashflow forecasting can push their level of certainty higher and help them move towards a happier life generally. It can be the catalyst towards a strong sense of wellbeing.

In our quest to introduce this concept to employees we have learned a lot, especially how not to do it! It was simply the most requested area of financial education from employees and we had to find a way to deliver it. Once employees had seen that the road to retirement, irrespective of their age now, was bumpy and that retirement will be potentially phased in and encompass a number of income sources, not just one pension scheme, a tool like a cashflow forecaster was the most useful way to simplify this complex situation.

We searched for what we thought was the best and most useful cashflow forecasting tool. In the UK alone there are around 15 different solutions available and we wanted to identify what we believed was the easiest to understand. I am sure there are lots that are good enough, I would suggest that you do some research and find one for your employees.

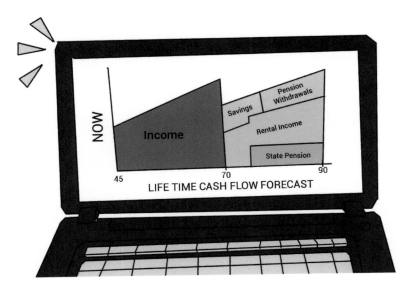

There are freebies available online but they are often too basic and the output is a little meaningless. Pension providers offer them as part of the group pension offering, but they are hardly used and most are only pension-product focused. There are others that we felt were just too complicated to understand.

Once we had selected a good cashflow forecasting tool we made sure that we had enough skilled operators and then we invited employees to tutorials to teach them to do it for themselves. They were very motivated because they had seen the concept at the 'awareness' stage and they were looking for their own financial certainty. After the tutorials they were signposted to the software provider who offered a free one-month trial period. So what went wrong?

Unfortunately the majority of attendees left their session very keen but when they tried to do it themselves they failed. We learned that unless they were using this software often and had a good financial background knowledge, they just got stuck and left frustrated. It really required a skilled operator.

At the next stage we tried to automate the process by sending employees an electronic fact finding document to complete (a simpler version than usual) and then we could pull that information into the software and generate an automatic 'example' cashflow report for them. This was a bold idea, however, it too fell over for two reasons.

Firstly, even though we had shortened and simplified the fact finding document, it still put people off. We only had around 20% returned. After speaking to a few employees we realised that the longer the employee left it to complete the less likely they were to ever complete it and send it back. Once the procrastination set in, it was too late as their desire waned over time too.

Secondly, we had to build a whole host of defaults and assumptions into this 'example' report, and what came out in many cases was somewhat meaningless. As everybody has their own view of how they want to live in the future there was no default position that catered for everybody. This was a good place for younger employees to start though, just to check they were heading in the right direction. However, it was not working for older employees.

We were determined not to give up, because this was by far the most requested aspect of financial education - and if you can find a way to make this work, your financial education programme will fly.

What we have found works really well is to send out the electronic fact finder and at the same time set up a turbo-meeting/skype/gotomeeting with a skilled operator of the software at a predetermined date and time in the future, usually about two weeks out. As there is now a deadline and a meeting booked for a chat with a skilled operator, employees have shown much more commitment to follow through with the fact finding.

We experienced a jump to around 70% returns. The fact find populates the software and this is then ready for the skilled operator and the employee to refine during their turbo-meeting. It usually takes around 15 minutes for the report to take shape and it often contains more than one strategy. It provides the employee with either certainty about their future, an early warning of potential problems to come or demonstrates the value of seeking some proper financial advice. Advice can appear costly when employees don't understand the value, but for many of them this clearly shows they would be wise to find some. Alternatively, their workplace financial education programme might do the trick for now.

If this is a step too far, you could discuss this with your employee benefits provider. They should have the expertise to provide the software and the skilled operator. It is well worth the effort, as over the last three years, this has been the most requested financial education topic among employees - but only after they have been presented with the concept, as prior to this most have not heard about the concept. It is one of the reasons a good 'awareness' strategy is so important. They now know what they need to know!

Relevant tutorials

Now that you've raised awareness about financial wellbeing and how to achieve it among your employees, the next step is subject-specific tutorials. You can go much deeper in terms of detail now because they have all self-selected the topic after the initial 'awareness' positioning and therefore it will be very relevant to them and usually their families. It is useful for larger firms to ask employees to list their tutorial requests in order of priority so that you can aim to deliver their most important ones first.

It is really important here to act fairly quickly too. After the initial awareness stage, the tutorials should be delivered as quickly as reasonably possible. We have experienced quite a significant drop out when we left the tutorials for more than a few weeks. It is difficult to know which topics will be most popular at each employer, as the employees are all different (apart from cashflow forecasting), but we have found that to allocate some time in the week following the initial awareness presentation works best. Too soon and they feel that they already spent quite a bit of time today or this week on financial education and would rather wait a little. Too late, i.e. more than a couple of weeks, and you find that the desire wears off and they can get distracted.

To administer the tutorials of various subjects, we would recommend that you involve your marketing team again and make use of their CRM system. It is important to know the number of registrations if these are run face-to-face as you need to know if the facilities can cope. You also want to be able to send out information in advance and take a register for MI purposes.

Top tips for tutorials

- Keep the groups small - aim for 10. If you set up 12 or 13 attendees, usually around 10 show up.
- Deliver in a sit-down conversational style around a table. Avoid a theatre-style room otherwise it feels like a lecture.
- Involve the attendees with exercises and practical takeaways. It's good for them to come away with something even if it is just a guide to the subject they have been learning about.
- If the subject is generally for younger employees, use younger tutorial facilitators. That is what younger employees have told us!
- Stick to morning sessions or over lunch. Drop-out rates are higher in the afternoons. Avoid Mondays and Fridays if possible too.
- If you do it over lunch, provide lunch and tell them to expect it. It becomes an extra motivation to attend.
- Make the facilitator available for half an hour after the session, there are always plenty of personal queries employees want to ask about.
- If advice is required, teach them how to find an adviser and what attributes to look for regarding that particular subject matter.
- Always link the content and learning to the employee benefits

package if relevant to get a better level of appreciation for the investment.

- Don't do tutorials about debt, no-one will show. It's too personal and taboo. Instead signpost them to your Employee Assistance Programme if you have one or to a charity that helps those in debt.
- Tutorials about mortgages require one-to-one sessions afterwards as a large proportion of the attendees want to discuss their own personal circumstances.
- Show employees how to increase their pension contributions at your firm. You will find many will want to after being educated.

Convert troublemakers into allies

There are situations where you get people with more than average knowledge about financial matters attending sessions, or where someone who is argumentative or cynical comes along and could make your tutorial into something of a battle. You want to avoid that at all costs, because it creates tension and detracts from the main point of the session: to educate people. But there are ways to turn someone like that into a real asset.

For example, I ran a session recently where the HR department warned me about a particular guy, and said he could be disruptive and argumentative. I got them to tell me his name, and to point him out to me when he arrived at the session. As it happened, he was the first to turn up, so I approached him, addressed him by name and started a conversation.

I told him I'd heard about him, and that he knew a lot about the topic we were going to be discussing. I encouraged him to share his knowledge with everyone else, because they wouldn't know as much as him and told him that by working together we could help everyone else learn something really valuable. His demeanour softened, he became much more engaged and he was a real asset to that session, because I'd empowered him to help others learn. That's a great example of where a personal connection can make a real difference.

You also need to ensure that you're helping people every step of the way. Often, you're dealing with intelligent people who might feel embarrassed that they need help with this aspect of their lives. As a financial educator, it's your job to reassure them that it's fine to ask for help. This isn't their specialism and they shouldn't be expected to know everything. You're guiding them through the process and making them feel comfortable, not only in tackling their finances, but also in asking for and receiving advice about them.

What's in a name?

What you label your tutorials can have a big impact not only on what numbers you get and who attends, but also on how people will approach the session. If you call them things like 'Estate Planning' or 'Retirement' it sets a certain tone, it doesn't sound exciting and it's not something people can relate to. These words are the features - we need to focus the employees on the benefits of the tutorials.

Again this is where your marketing team can help carefully craft the titles to attract employees. Rather than 'Estate Planning Tutorial' how about, 'Who's Going To End Up With Your Money?' The title demonstrates the value and the benefits of attending. It can be very emotive and that's the reason people want to attend.

Instead of 'Pension Tutorial' how about, 'How to achieve the retirement of your dreams', or, 'Your guide to modern day retirement planning'. Instead of, 'Budgeting Tutorial', how about, 'How to take control of your finances for a better life'. I think you get the gist of it now! It pays to be a little creative here and push out the benefits to employees.

Always, always, always provide solutions

One thing you have to be very careful of when you're running a financial wellbeing strategy is that people don't leave your sessions worrying about things. You can be raising awareness of some pretty terrifying situations and you can be making people aware of problems they didn't realise they had. What you really don't want is for people to become paralysed by that fear or anxiety.

You always need to counter any anxiety you might induce with plenty of positivity and provide people with real solutions that they can work on themselves. You might think you've given people that hope that they can improve their situation, but often their biggest worry is knowing they need to fix something but not having the resources to fix it.

We always recommend that you have a section at the end of every tutorial about how to find a financial adviser. The majority won't need or want advice at this stage, most are very satisfied that they are now very aware and can make most changes themselves. But for the few that do, give them information and training about the attributes they should look for in a relevant adviser to the subject in hand and point them towards search websites for financial advisers, as well as explaining how the advice can be funded.

Linking financial education to employee benefits

Whenever you're delivering this detailed level of financial education, you need to be mindful of linking it back to employer offerings. Most people are totally unaware of all the benefits their employer provides them with and therefore don't make use of them.

If people don't understand them, or aren't aware of them, they aren't going to value these benefits and as an employer that's not good news, because you're probably paying a fair bit for your benefits package. Consider running tutorials on the employee benefits package itself and link the benefits to the various different subjects in your financial education programme, it works both ways.

The job in hand is to educate people about finances in general, about specific aspects that contribute to their financial wellbeing. Things like avoiding debt, how to get a good mortgage deal, preparing for retirement, organising their inheritance and so on, and about how their employer can help them on their journey to becoming financially free.

For instance, if you look at financial protection, products like income protection, life insurance and critical illness cover, most people haven't thought properly about that. They don't understand why it's relevant to them and getting that emotive connection with a dry financial product is a large part of your job. But once they understand the value of it, you can make an incredibly positive emotional connection to the employee by pointing out that three-quarters of their needs are covered by their benefits package at work.

Finding out about a potential issue and understanding the repercussions of not having those financial products in place can be stressful, but if you can immediately counter that with the relief of discovering they're already covered, it's incredibly powerful and the positive emotions linked to that sense of relief are directed at the organisation providing that security - namely their employer.

Employees are retiring later

Pensions are another big thing to link back to employers, especially because the pension scheme is usually the most expensive benefit that any employer provides. But education around pensions has got worse since the new pension freedoms were introduced two years ago, and it's a problem that needs addressing.

Where people are now allowed to withdraw their pension in a lump sum at 55, rather than taking an annuity, there's a real danger that they'll spend it and run out of money. While that's a big problem for the person who's spent their pension savings, it's just as big a problem for employers. There's no mandatory retirement age any more, which means, in theory, people can work for as long as they like.

If you have employees who, at 55, are withdrawing their pension savings, spending them and then continuing to work into their 70s because they need the cash, you're potentially going to end up with an ageing workforce and be unable to introduce new, young talent because so many people are working later and later in life. Now there's nothing wrong with people working into their 70s if they still have the desire and drive to do so, but if you have people of that age working simply because they need the money, you're more likely to encounter problems.

Making sure all your employees are properly educated about the pension scheme you're providing them with is vital. But you also need to target those nearing retirement age to ensure they understand what their options are when it comes to drawing their pension, and the potential impact of choosing one option over another. You can't tell people what to do, but by making sure they're educated about their financial situation and have that financial security, you'll be helping them make positive decisions about their future.

The Final Step To Financial Freedom

5

As an employer, you want your financial wellbeing strategy to be overwhelmingly positive for your employees, which means there's one final step you may need to take once you've educated them: delivery. Prior to the financial education programme, they may have been happily ignorant to the things they need to do and the next steps they need to take to move towards a sense of financial freedom. Now though, they will be very aware of the most important next step for them. If they cannot find a way of taking that next step with ease and affordably, this could create new stress.

In an ideal world every employee would engage the services of a trusted financial adviser who would coach them regularly to achieve all of their financial objectives and protect them from every potential financial problem that could present itself to them. Unfortunately we do not live in an ideal world, in fact we are a million miles away from that ideal.

For all the reasons stated in the introduction to this book regarding the supply and demand for advice, a new terminology has been created - the advice gap. It is basically the difference between the cost of advice and the amount people are willing to pay. The vast majority of employees will never be able to afford advice. But interestingly, most don't understand the value anyway because they have not been educated in this area.

When an employer delivers a good-quality financial education programme they inadvertently exacerbate the problem by educating employees into the 'advice gap'. They were there before but totally unaware, now they are very aware and this could be a cause for concern and defeat the very reason for educating them in the first place, to reduce stress and anxiety!

This leaves employers with a conundrum, educate and risk further worry due to a lack of ability to solve the problems OR don't educate and leave them in the very place we have already said is not working. The advice gap is very real, and is especially a problem for people with small pension pots who can't afford advice but need it to access their pensions!

Onerous regulation is the main reason; it makes the advice process and the advice liability so strong that the price for advice is simply out of reach for the vast majority of employees. However, help is at hand. Many employers have some solutions to some of these problems right under their noses!

Bridging the advice gap

We now have a large number of employees well educated and requiring some solutions to fulfil their requirements financially. We have worked with a number of employers to construct a 'bridge' over this advice gap. If we were building a real bridge we would use building blocks. Many of these building blocks are actually resources that are already available to employees but they are invisible to them. Some are contained within the existing employee benefits package, some are free-of-charge external resources, some are new-to-market solutions that haven't taken off yet and some are simply much more affordable and creative ways of actually paying for advice.

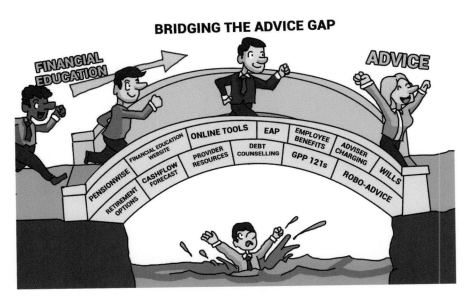

BRIDGING THE ADVICE GAP

As an employer it is useful to take a look at which of these building blocks you already have, it just may be that when they were last promoted your employees were simply not financially educated and therefore they missed them, remember RAS? It could be that the employee benefits communication is ineffective or non-existent. It could just be that the communication of such things has gone stale and employees have stopped noticing.

Obviously a good financial education strategy can bring those things back to life which is great for ROI, but there is so much more that can be done without the employer spending another penny. There are even solutions within benefits packages that employers are unaware of. If we identify all of these resources plus what is available externally, often for free, we have the building blocks to bridge the gap.

The building blocks to bridge the gap

Government and charity resources

There are a number of organisations that can help employees by providing financial guidance. It is only guidance and should not be confused with advice but for many it is more than sufficient for their needs. Such organisations include:

- **The Money Advice Service**. They are mainly focused on supporting people with debt problems now, and they have a useful website.
- **The Pension Regulator.** Part of the government's Pension Wise solution. They provide a telephone-based guidance service for those considering cashing in their pension since the introduction of pensions freedoms.
- **Citizens Advice.** Also part of the government's Pension Wise solution. They have been helping people for many years with all aspects of financial guidance. More recently they have been providing the face-to-face guidance for Pension Wise.

Pension provider online tools and resources

In their quest to increase funds under management and prevent the larger pots from transferring away at retirement, the pension industry is evolving all the time to add more value to their policyholders. They can offer online pension targeting tools, investment risk analysis, portfolio construction, consolidation services and even pension educational roadshows and financial guidance services.

As an employer it is worth noting their main drivers, which mean there will always be a bias as their guidance will only usually be towards their own products. But this is not a reason to not take advantage of what they have to offer. For many lower-paid employees with smaller pension pots, this may be their only option. They can also offer, for a fee, an ongoing guidance service. It's definitely a solution to consider but if you do, compare their costs for guidance because in many cases employees can actually get independent regulated advice elsewhere for the same price.

Nudge is an online financial education business, and research contained in their Financial Education Yearbook 2016/17 pointed out that 96% of employers surveyed want their financial education to be independent of pension and product providers, yet currently only 18% is!

Retirement options reports

For older employees who have smaller pension pots and cannot justify or afford to pay for regulated advice, there are automated solutions, independent of pension providers, who can, for a small fee, produce a retirement strategy report. Taking into account their pension assets and the individual's objectives it can calculate the most appropriate annuity and/or flexible pension withdrawal strategy. Talk to your employee benefits advisers as they will be able to help you with one. This is probably one of the most important things an employer could introduce for the vast majority of employees because there are around 700,000 people retiring each year with average pot sizes of around £50,000. They often just take the first retirement strategy that they are offered, usually by their pension provider.

Mortgage services

After death in the family and divorce, moving house is generally accepted as the third biggest cause of stress. Many people try and find their own mortgage or remortgage on the internet, it's the first place they go. However, these DIY mortgagees can be a problem. Research conducted by Which? magazine in 2015 said that the average person spent eight hours researching mortgages online. And only one in four got the right mortgage deal. What a waste of time and money. Plus, many of them probably conducted their research whilst at work!

To solve this, you could introduce a mortgage education and/or advice service. There are a number of firms that specialise in this service and they do it for free. They set up a training session and then offer individual one-to-one sessions with a specialist mortgage adviser on the same day. When they are offered at employers with an online registration system they are nearly always oversubscribed.

Helping employees with debt

There are a number of specialist firms that may be able to help employees. They can offer and facilitate access to affordable borrowing that can be repaid directly from their salaries. They are well worth a look because this is such a stressful topic for employees to deal with and this may provide a credible plan to get out of their current painful situation and into a place that will help their overall wellbeing. Simply having a light at the end of the tunnel will positively impact their happiness.

A cashflow forecast service

We have already mentioned this as part of a life plan to help create a sense of financial freedom for employees in the previous chapter. If you can find a way to achieve a simple and cost-effective solution, this will form an enormous building block in your bridge over the advice gap.

Employee Assistance Programmes (EAP)

An EAP is an employee benefit that assists employees with personal problems or work-related problems that may impact their performance, health, mental, financial or emotional wellbeing. EAPs generally offer free and confidential assessments, short-term counselling, referrals, and follow-up services for employees and their families. Even though EAPs are mainly aimed at work-related problems, there are a variety of programs that can assist with problems outside of the workplace.

From the perspective of bridging the advice gap, EAPs can play an important role in supporting employees with money worries. Many offer telephone counselling, others will even offer face-to-face counselling, all totally confidential so employees needn't worry about their employer finding out about personal circumstances. Here is the problem: they are simply not used enough. The number of calls to an EAP provider is exceptionally low in percentage terms as employees are often unaware that they exist.

There is one more interesting fact: Many employers have an EAP but they just do not know it! Many group risk products such as group life assurance and group income protection offer this for free. They are poorly promoted because the low call figures keep the cost down for the insurer whilst still maintaining a very impressive product feature.

The message here is to go and talk to your provider and see what you already have. I have experienced a situation where an employer was paying separately for an EAP that they already had as a feature within their group income protection policy. They switched off the external product and used the money savings on other employee benefits.

Will writing service

This costs employers nothing. Research from Money Marketing magazine in 2015 concluded that over half of UK adults do not have a will - an important item for the financial security of employees and their families. There are plenty of law firms offering workplace solutions at group discounted rates and you could consider payroll-deducted payment arrangements. These firms will also be keen to come to your premises and train employees on the subject.

Tax returns service

As with will writing services, there are plenty of tax returns services available but most employers do not include them in their suite of benefits. They have become much more important since 2016 because of the new rules around pension contribution allowances being affected by a new definition of income called 'adjusted income'.

More higher-earning employees now than ever before will want to utilise unused pension allowances through their tax returns to minimise their tax liabilities caused by the new rules.

Employee financial advice options

Financial advice in the workplace has become almost non-existent since the indemnity commission from group pensions was abolished over the last few years. This has come at a time when I have never seen the importance of financial advice so strong due to many of the factors described in the introductory chapters in this book. Employers' views on financial advice for employees are often polarised and can be swayed away from it now that they might have to pay for it.

Cost aside, one of the other reasons for those choosing not to get involved has been the risk attached to it. If there was no risk to the employer and no cost, all employers would probably want to offer it as the pros outweigh the cons.

Nowadays there are many ways to help employees access regulated financial advice and the risk is not quite as worrying as some employers might think. The main thing you need to remember in terms of risk is that legally, there is actually zero risk if you are only introducing an adviser that works independently of product providers. If you engage a responsible and high-quality firm of financial advisers and put your employees in contact with them, that relationship is entirely between the individuals who pay for financial advice and the firm supplying it. Your business is removed from all liability if they are a regulated firm.

Where there is a risk, it is to your reputation if something goes wrong. But this can be minimised by ensuring the financial advisers you work with are experienced and provide an excellent service. The reputational risk generally lies with service delivery, rather than the quality of the advice itself. You don't want people to go to a firm you've recommended, only to have a poor experience. That breaks trust, which you've been building throughout this whole process, both with the financial adviser and your business.

But if the financial advisers you work with treat your employees with respect, care about their individual needs and problems and deliver an excellent service, it will strengthen that bond. If you use a firm of advisers to help with your financial education programme they would be well positioned to help your employees because that all important element of trust has already begun to build. You could provide them with a copy of this book to help them make sure the programme is delivered as effectively as possible.

Later in this chapter we will take a look at the attributes to look for in an adviser firm that will help minimise the reputational risk. If the perceived risk can be reduced significantly it may reach a point when you as an employer are prepared to go for it because, on balance, the upside benefits outweigh the downside reputational risks.

You can introduce a training module, or add something to existing tutorials that will teach employees how to find a good, affordable adviser to meet their needs. Most people see advisers as all the same, but they are not. They vary in qualifications, experience and specialisms. It's about matching and deploying the right adviser to the right employee profile and need. If you owned a brand new Rolls Royce car you wouldn't go to a tyre fitter to get the car serviced. Equally, if you owned a cheap run-around car you wouldn't go to the Rolls Royce dealership for a new tyre.

Ways to provide advice for employees

Robo-advice

This is a very modern concept that will eventually settle into its rightful position as a building block for the bridge over the advice gap. There are a number of websites that offer what is known as robo-advice. They are struggling at present to work profitably but as an industry we are all hoping that they will fill that all important gap and deliver affordable solutions.

ROBO - ADVICE

There are two main problems: Firstly they do not give advice. They facilitate an investment outcome and are very slick, but they do not provide any sort of relationship or influence people in any way. Secondly, before an individual goes to one of these websites, they must have already been influenced, positioned, educated and know exactly what investment outcome they desire.

The emotional decision has to have been made to do something before they get started. People will not go to the website unless they have a problem they are aware of to solve and they know how to solve it. This is the fundamental problem with robo-advice. However, this is where workplace financial education can work really well. The education programme can be the very thing that educates and positions employees providing the necessary motivation to go to the robo-adviser and transact an investment.

Group Personal Pension advice

This was very popular at the pension enrolment stage for new employees when it was funded by indemnity commission from the pension provider. Pension automatic enrolment and the abolition of commission has pretty much killed this off. Some employers still like to offer this and they pay for it, but they are in the minority. It is a great way to get a strong ROI for the most expensive employee benefit and delivers a high degree of employee engagement and wellbeing. If an employer pays for it there will be tax implications to consider.

You could offer an advice service that the employee pays for themselves. If the value of the advice is presented well there are definitely employees who are happy to pay a small fee. This could be made easier if the employer pays up front and deducts from the employee's pay over the year. However, by far the most popular way is for the advice to be paid for by way of what is known as 'adviser charging'. This little known option is covered in more detail on page 101. There are quite a few smaller firms that can deliver this type of service. Look for ones that have a number of employee benefits clients. Generally the larger employee benefits consultancies are not geared up for this type of work.

Helping your employees engage a financial adviser

If you decide not to work closely with a financial advisory firm to bridge this advice gap - or even if you do but want to make sure your employees have all the options - you need to give them some guidance about how to find a reputable financial adviser on their own.

People are scared of sticking a pin in a phone book and going to any old firm. They need someone they trust, someone who will listen to their concerns and needs and put their best interests at heart. Ideally, they'd choose an adviser based on a personal recommendation from a friend or colleague, but that's not always possible.

There are two levels of trust that people look for in a financial adviser. The first is in competence and capability. *Do they have the expertise to help me, are they compliant with the regulator and do they get results?* The second is trust in character. *Do they have the right values and will they put my interests first?*

You need both aspects of this trust to be strong for a successful relationship to develop. If there's already a corporate relationship between the financial adviser and the employer you're more likely to trust them, especially if that firm is involved in running the financial education programme and you've interacted with them on some level, but don't underestimate the importance of making that personal connection too. A good adviser will build trust by simply asking the right questions. You should judge an adviser on the quality of the questions they ask and their ability to listen, rather than their qualifications alone.

To give you a case in point, I'll tell you about a top adviser that I know personally. He was in a three-man competition to obtain a very wealthy client. My chap was eventually selected by the client. When he asked what the difference was between him and the other two advisers who were vying for the business, the client told him that the other advisers simply talked about their clever, sophisticated investment solutions, whereas our adviser asked questions about his personal objectives and financial goals.

His first question was, "What's important to you about money?" And then when he had the answer, he followed up with, "And what's important about that?" By asking those questions he was getting to the core of what was important to the client - his family and his future - rather than showing off about his own capabilities. The client felt like our adviser had his best interests at heart, and that built a level of trust that the other two firms couldn't compete with.

So the main advice for your employees is to work with a financial adviser they trust. They need to look for someone who puts them at the centre of their solution.

Identifying a firm of financial advisers to support your employees

Aside from the worry over the risk of providing financial advice to your employees through a recommended firm, one of the main barriers for businesses is actually finding an organisation that they are comfortable working with.

You need to be thorough in your assessment of any financial advisers you're considering working with to deliver that final and all-important step of your financial wellbeing strategy, and you need to know exactly what to look for in a reputable firm.

The Top 10 Attributes To Look For In An Adviser For Your Employees

1 The first thing you need to consider is coverage. Where are your employees based and will the firms you're considering be in a position to provide face-to-face interactions with the majority of them? While in person is the best option where possible, online can work as well provided the organisation in question has a robust online meeting solution. Remember the importance of using video calling and webcasts. Talking over the phone is rarely enough.

2 You need to ask whether the firm has a centralised advice process, because any firm that says yes will be able to provide a degree of consistency. What you don't want is for two people who work together to have wildly different experiences of the same company, because that will cause resentment from the person who feels like they received the worse experience. Everything needs to be uniform in how they deal with your employees; you need to know the organisation is providing high-quality, incredibly consistent and uniformly priced advice.

3 Good credentials and a strong reputation are the next things to look for. Have a good look at their website, but don't forget to see what the individual financial advisers within that company are doing. Look up their LinkedIn profiles, see what they're talking about and what endorsements they have. You want to dig a little deeper than their qualifications. Find out what their specialities, passions and values are.

4 Industry recognition is similar, but a valuable thing to look for when building up a picture of a firm. Ask other businesses in the same sector what they think of the firm(s) you're considering working with, and check to see if they've won any recent awards or have consistently won awards for their services. Working with an organisation that has a strong brand will help your employees trust the advisers you're using, and will give them confidence in the service they're receiving.

5 Compliance is also key, as are the systems and controls a business has in place. Always ask if a firm is directly regulated through the regulator, or whether they go through a network. Also find out if they have a compliance department. Smaller firms may not have the resources for an entire department, but they should at least have an individual in the business who has a control function known as CF10. Essentially this makes them the compliance director or manager for that business, and they will have taken an oath with the regulator to uphold standards.

6   Get references from clients, past and present. What you're looking for are those raving fan clients. Satisfied clients are great, but they won't promote a business. You want to see that a firm has these fans. Ask them for references. One who is a corporate client that they have a strong relationship with and one previous client. Always try to speak to people directly on the phone when you're getting a reference. People aren't always happy about putting things in writing, and are likely to be much more open about their experiences if you can get them in conversation.

7   You need to see how they deal with complaints and if they've had any in the past, what they've done since to tackle the problem. You need to look at their advice process and make sure it will work for your employees and that you're happy with it from a standards point of view.

8   Is cashflow forecasting at the centre of their proposition? I've talked about the importance of this in delivering a tailored and valuable financial wellbeing strategy and you need to find a financial adviser who recognises its value and is prepared to offer that to all your employees, not just the high earners.

9   Avoid working with tied advisers. This is incredibly important because tied advisers are more like salespeople than advisers. They are paid to sell products and that creates bias. They won't work on behalf of their clients, and therefore won't be working on behalf of your employees - they're working on behalf of their firm. Always choose an independent or restricted adviser. Don't be put off by the term 'restricted adviser', this simply means that rather than being totally independent they have a centralised investment proposition. Their advice won't be biased by the options within that proposition, so they're independent in that they help each client do the best thing for their individual situation. The advantage to restricted advisers is that they'll have become experts in a range of different investments within this centralised proposition, rather than trying to become an expert in every single investment option available on the market. Usually, having a group of investments also means they can control the price down on behalf of the employee, govern the investment returns and alter this proposition as time progresses.

10 Client relationship management. The main complaint about advisers is that due to the sometimes lengthy advice process, things can go quiet and clients suspect that the adviser is slow or has forgotten about them. Make sure they have a way of staying in touch regularly.

Adviser charging - how to bring advice to a larger number of employees

This is a very important building block for the advice bridge. Adviser charging allows employees to access financial advice without having to pay for it directly from net pay; they can pay for it from their gross pension pots instead. This feature is available in different guises through a large number of group pension providers but is currently little known in the workplace. The fee agreed with the adviser is paid by way of a deduction from the pension pot - in our experience around 80% of pension advice is paid for in this way.

Not all pension providers offer this and some will only work with advisers that they have pre-approved. However, if you can get this to work on the back end of a financial education programme you will experience very positive take up of advice services, which will go a long way to enhancing the overall wellbeing of those employees.

A financial concierge service

There are many building blocks available to help bridge the advice gap and there should be a solution for most problems for most employees. However, the sheer amount of choice can be a problem in itself. What we have found that works really well is to appoint an individual within your HR team, or outsource to your employee benefits adviser, who is a go-to person that your employees can talk to about the financial issues they need help with. They can act as a kind of financial concierge for your employees and can triage and signpost employees to the most appropriate solution.

Obviously they should possess some basic financial knowledge, but more importantly have a good knowledge of all the solutions - the building blocks - available to your employees. Their job is to help achieve the optimum outcome for employees. You can promote this service internally with a dedicated helpline number and if you have a web-based/intranet financial education site you can promote it there too. This will also act as a great tool to enhance the appreciation of the employee benefits package that you offer.

How to create a budget for financial education

You may already have a budget for employee benefits communication and pension education, or you may be fortunate enough to have an employee wellbeing budget. Financial wellbeing falls somewhere between the two; it really depends on how each individual employer chooses to view it. However, as wellbeing programmes and financial education programmes are a relatively new concept it is highly likely that you do not have a budget. And you may have to wait a year to get one as budgets may have been set for the year at your firm.

One way to create some spare cash is to offer your pension scheme on a 'salary sacrifice' or 'salary exchange' basis. This is by no means a new concept, in fact most SMEs and large corporates already offer this to their employees. But how does this help you? The original employee 'exchanged' contribution becomes an employer pension contribution and therefore does not require employers' National Insurance (NIC) to be paid. This currently stands at 13.8% and therefore can create significant monetary savings. E.g. a 500 employee firm, with an average salary of £30,000 with a 5% matched pension contribution would save £103,500 per annum if there were no opt-outs of the pension or the salary exchange offer.

While the majority of employers prefer to share some or all of the saving by way of an increased pension contribution into the employees' pots, even sharing the NIC saving 50/50 would save, in this example, over £50,000 per annum.

Too late, we have done it already

You may be thinking that you already have a salary exchange arrangement set up and the savings have already been absorbed into the business accounts. In this situation, it is useful to increase the employer NIC savings by encouraging employees to save more – and this is where your financial education programme can pay for itself.

We can use the same example: 500 employees, average income £30,000 with a 5% matched pension contribution and 100% enrolment. If the education has worked well the average employee would, from our experience, increase their personal contributions from between 1% to 5%. If we assumed an average increase of just 2% of salary and a 50/50 share of the NIC saving, the employer would save £20,700.

This could then become your annual budget for all the other aspects of your financial education programme. In this example, you would be amazed at how much financial education value can be achieved with this sort of money. And once it has been pledged it can potentially become a permanent employee benefit investment.

There is one thing to consider here though, and that is salary exchange for pension contributions may not be available forever. We have seen recently that its use for childcare vouchers and 'bikes to work' has been abolished. It would be a massive upheaval for most benefits programmes but I wouldn't be surprised to see salary exchange on pension contributions disappear over the next few years as well. We will have to watch this space.

Even if you made the savings for just a few years and reinvested them in improving the financial wellbeing of your employees, you may have other increased productivity and reduced employee turnover measurables that could easily justify the investment going forward.

Redirection of budget from other employee benefits

After pensions, the most expensive employee benefits are Group Income Protection (GIP), Group Life Assurance and Private Healthcare. It is worth talking to your broker because many of these products are renewed at the last minute and certain aspects are often overlooked.

Each year they usually benefit from a unit rate review, but are not always reviewed from a product structure perspective. Take the time to examine these products, as you could make significant savings. Look at the percentage increase on the income in payment and make sure it reflects the current economy – bringing this down could save up to 20%.

Changing the pay-out terms to reflect the average claim which is less than five years, instead of paying out until age 65, could reduce the cost by as much as 50%. Early intervention of GIP claims by the healthcare provider can help get employees back to work before a GIP claim is made, thus minimising claims which will help control or reduce annual premiums, as well as providing better continuity in work.

Paying a set fee rather than a commission can also reduce overall costs as the broker is more motivated to get the premium down, i.e. there is no detriment to their earnings. In the case of private healthcare this can also reduce tax for both the employer and the employee.

Restricting the conditions covered on a Critical Illness policy to those which are more common will also bring costs down. In addition, with private healthcare you could raise the excess, implement a cap on outpatient therapy and reduce the hospital list to exclude the top London hospitals, which will all help to reduce the annual costs.

The bottom line here is to review your group risk products properly. It might be useful to invite another couple of brokers to take a look with a fresh set of eyes and this will certainly keep your current broker honest.

Take stock again

Depending on what stage you are at in your programme, you may have completed it, you should re-run your original financial wellbeing survey and compare it to where you were at the start of the project. Hopefully, you will have made good progress and improved the financial wellbeing of your employees. You can also take a look at the NPS from throughout the programme and together this will provide useful MI for you to tweak your strategy.

If you are planning to do more, this will enable you to focus your time and energy in a more strategic way and optimise your outcome. Taking stock and producing some concrete data will help you justify the time, energy and expense of the project to the business. It will also go a long way to helping secure further or continued investment. If you have a flexible benefits platform, you can measure the amount of engagement with it during the flex window period and attribute that to a new level of employee financial knowledge.

It is also worth looking at the specific tutorial requests from employees to gain an understanding of what is important to them right now, which will again help you with direction and strategy of resource going forward.

Summary

Financial education may not change your employees' financial position straight away, but it can improve their psychology very quickly. To have light at the end of the tunnel, to have a plan for life, to anticipate potential threats early on, to know that there is help if they need it all goes a long way towards helping them feel that sense of financial freedom that we all want. It has been said many times that knowledge is power and in this situation it really is and it can provide a strong financial wellbeing foundation to build upon.

It becomes an on-going requirement as the world, business, globalisation, legislation, governments, attitudes and expectations are changing all the time and a financial education programme has to develop at the same speed. So there will always be something to educate about, it is a journey rather than a destination. This even applies to retirement - it used to be a day in the future that all work ends; now it has become a very flexible arrangement with multiple income sources.

As an employer who dedicates themselves to enhancing the financial wellbeing of your employees you will set yourself apart from the rest, your employees will feel engaged and connected in a whole new way. It won't be just a job anymore; it will become a part of their life, an important part that they will cherish more deeply – all of which will help towards having a highly engaged, productive and functional workforce.

You will be surprised when you take a look at the number of employees who go through your programme, and as long as you have conducted it in accordance with the contents of this book, you will find that this will be your most successful employee engagement exercise ever! I challenge you to give it a go.

I'm passionate about the difference financial wellbeing can make to people's lives, and you can contact me to find out more about how to harness the power of a financially free workforce for your business: **01932 871355** or **darren.laverty@second-sight.com**

Recommended Reading

This book focuses primarily on how to implement a successful financial education strategy, therefore I thoroughly recommend CIPD research findings available at the link below as a complementary read. This will allow you to further explore the 'why' and 'what' related to this content and offer you a greater understanding of the wider subject.

www.cipd.co.uk/financialwellbeing

About The Author

Darren Laverty is one of the UK's leading financial services performers and one of the Founding Partners at national financial advisory firm Foster Denovo, and Secondsight its employee benefits division. His passion is financial education and having dedicated the last 3 decades to this field, he is as excited about it today as the day he started out in 1988. Working with some of the UK's most impressive employers, Darren combines his vast expertise with this natural ability to communicate highly technical information in simple, visual terms so that people of all professions and backgrounds can learn with ease.

When Darren is not advising his clients, he is speaking at industry events and running educational seminars, workshops and webcasts to provide his network with the information they need to truly improve the lives of their employees. It is Darren's firm belief that there is no better way to engage than to provide empowering information delivered in a fun format and staying true to his unique approach, this book is no exception!

Darren Laverty and Secondsight have learned so much over the years that he is now delighted to be able to share it with employers and other financial educators in Make Their Money Count.

In addition to his work at Secondsight, Darren fundraises for two schools in Kenya, The Amani Junior Academy and the Showers of Blessings Academy, to help buy much needed text books and classroom desks. All profits from the sales of his book go directly to these 2 schools.

Darren Laverty lives in Windsor with his wife and two teenage children.

Our Fundraising

Secondsight regularly fundraises for good causes. Two of the good causes that are very close to our heart came about after Darren Laverty and his family visited Kenya in the Summer of 2011.

He saw for himself the hardship families go through in order to send their children to school, something that we take for granted in the UK, and pledged to support two schools once he returned to the UK.

The Amani Junior Academy & the Showers of Blessings Academy provide education for 5 to 16 years olds in the region of Watamu, a two hour drive north of Mombasa, Kenya. The schools provide an excellent level of education but pupils often lack the resources to buy basic items, such as textbooks, pencils and even classroom desks.

Our fundraising effort began at Employee Benefits Live 2011, where for every enquiry form completed at our stand we pledged one text book to the schools, and these efforts continue. Our progress so far:

Amani Junior Academy

Their aim for the Amani Junior Academy is to obtain 95 classroom desks and build a classroom. We have delivered 59 classroom desks so far.

Showers of Blessings Academy

Showers of Blessings Academy's aim is to provide 1700 textbooks. We have delivered 928 and 32 classroom desks.

To find out more about The Amani Junior Academy & the Showers of Blessings Academy and learn how you, too, can get involved, please visit our website or contact Darren directly:

http://www.second-sight.com/fundraising/
darren.laverty@second-sight.com

All profits from sale of this book will go directly to these two schools. Every book sold will buy a textbook, four books sold will pay for a classroom desk. Darren also provides a copy of this book free of charge and a classroom desk for one of the schools in Kenya for every genuine inquiry and subsequent meeting he has with firms exploring financial education for their employees

18227510R00077

Printed in Poland
by Amazon Fulfillment
Poland Sp. z o.o., Wrocław